The Easiest and Fastest Way To Manage Project of Any Types and Sizes

Project Management
Step-by-Step
Templates

- ➤ **5 Easy Steps** and **9 Success Keys** To Complete Your Project Successfully
- ➤ **Over 100** Templates, Flowcharts and Project Documents
- ➤ **Save Time** and **Money**
- ➤ For **Any Types** of Project

MARVIN M. GAMBOA, CE, PMP

Project Management
Step-by-Step Templates

By: Marvin M. Gamboa, CE,PMP

PROJECT MANAGEMENT:
STEP-BY-STEP TEMPLATES

ISBN: 978-971-95901-7-0

PIER ENGINEERING and CONSULTANTS

Project Managers ● Consulting Engineers

#0754, Zone 5, Maliwalo
Tarlac City, Philippines
+63(045) 491-4994
www.PierEngineeringandConsultants.com
info@pierengineeringandconsultants.com

Legal information and disclaimer: All the contents and information contained here are from author's knowledge, trainings and experiences, the purchaser of this publication assumes full responsibility for the use of this Book. This publication does not constitute legal and financial advice and the example project, format, document and data here are not intended to represent or guarantee that everyone in project management will achieve same results.

The condition of project will vary from region to region and from one country to another, it is highly recommended that the purchaser of this publication will consult professional, legal and professional authorities based on their project geographical area. Any legal templates and document here must be reviewed by legal professionals and authorities in your project location.

Contents

INTRODUCTION   1

STEP 1   Initiating   4

STEP 2   Planning   18

STEP 3   Executing   86

STEP 4   Monitoring and Controlling   137

STEP 5   Closing   174

TRAINING   Manage Templates and Documents the Easy Way   183

RESOURCES   188

Introduction

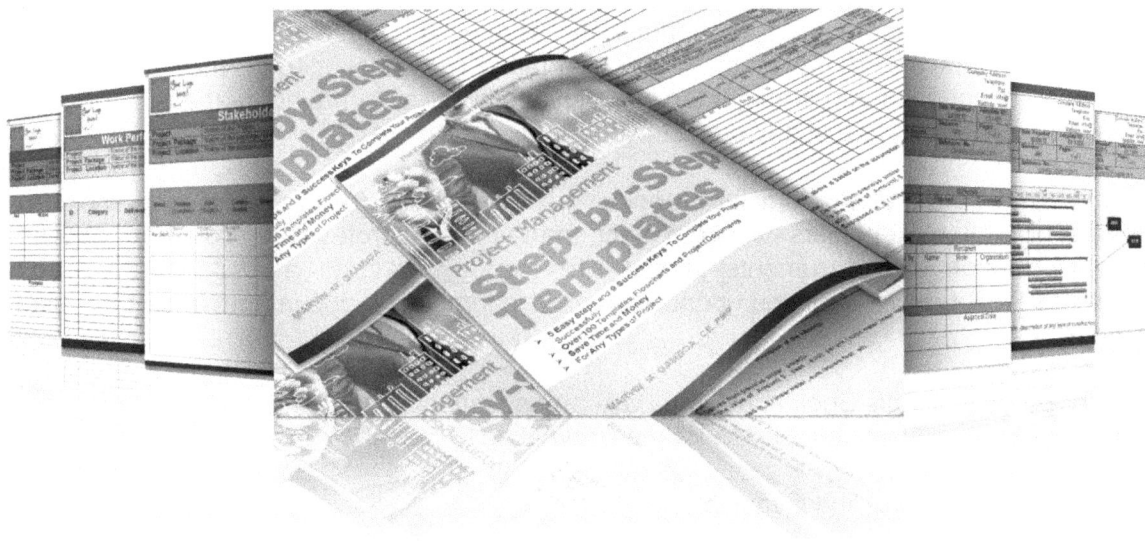

Welcome!

Welcome to Project Management: Step-by-Step Templates. In this Book we are going to talk about the 5 Easy steps and 9 success keys to manage different projects like IT, pharmaceutical, construction project and more.

The purpose of this publication is to present the applicable group of processes, procedures and techniques from project management standards for projects in a simplified and direct approach in a set of steps, keys, templates, forms, flow charts, documents and checklists with these set of tools, projects can be delivered easier, faster and safer to project owner.

I am a Certified Project Manager (PMP) and a registered Civil Engineer (CE). I have been in the construction industry for more than 15 years now, from junior to senior engineer up to project management level, I have seen project managers that failed and succeeded for their projects. It takes right knowledge, experience and the right tools to achieve success in project management, this Book will guide and help you succeed in any projects you handle.

I have numerous free templates, articles, reports, guides and tips for project management to help professionals or any stakeholders within project management profession. You can access free templates, information and documents in our site Pier Engineering and Consultants you can bookmark it and RSS feed to keep you updated for all free templates, documents and other resources for your projects.

Thank you for purchasing this Book and if you have any questions, comments and feedback, good or bad, I would love to hear from you, please let me know at send me info.

I hope it would be helpful and find it valuable.

To Your Project Success,

Marvin M. Gamboa

Who can use Project Management: A Complete Guide and Templates?

The primary audience to this publication is the project manager for any projects, to help them manage the project from start to hand over and from simple to complex projects. This publication can also be used but not limited to Managers, Engineers, Architects, Project Owner, General Contractor, Contractor and Sub-contractor, Builder, Supplier and Manufacturer, Project Authorities, Students, Project Management related professionals and any other stakeholders for any projects.

Project Management

Project Management is the use of knowledge, skills, tools and processes to deliver the specified project requirements. Project management as a whole is composed of 9 success keys or commonly known as knowledge areas and the 5 Easy Steps or the 5 process groups.

Project – A project is a TEMPORARY endeavor to produce a UNIQUE results, service or product.

- Temporary aspect of project is that, project has a definite start and end.
- Unique – project can produce unique characteristics, there is no exactly the same product or results in terms of time, location, circumstances, situation, type of materials, ownership and so on.

PROJECT MANAGEMENT STEPS

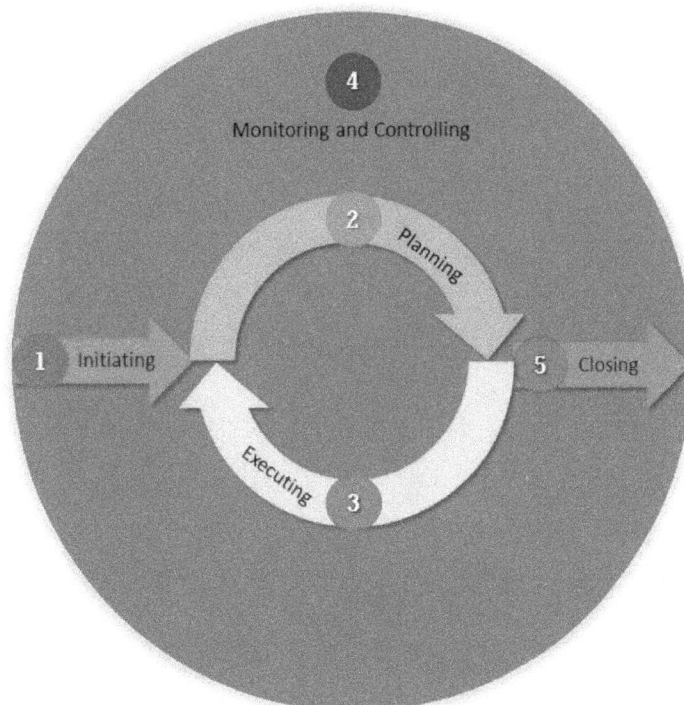

Step 1

Initiating

STEP 1 : INITIATING

Initiating is the first step in managing projects. It is composed of processes aimed to authorize the project, identify specific phases, determine stakeholders, assign project manager(s), and formally start the project work.

Flow Chart :

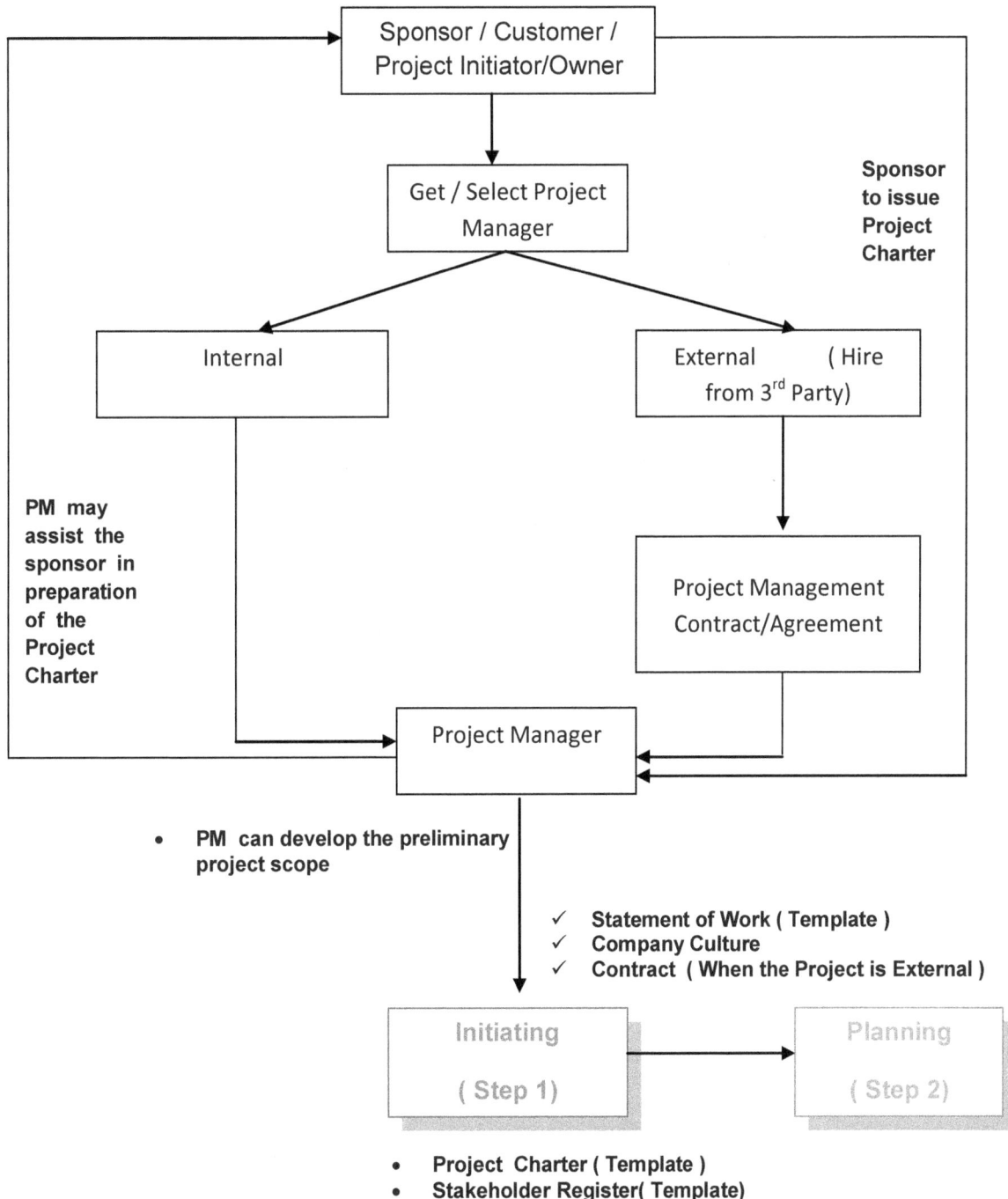

Mapping:

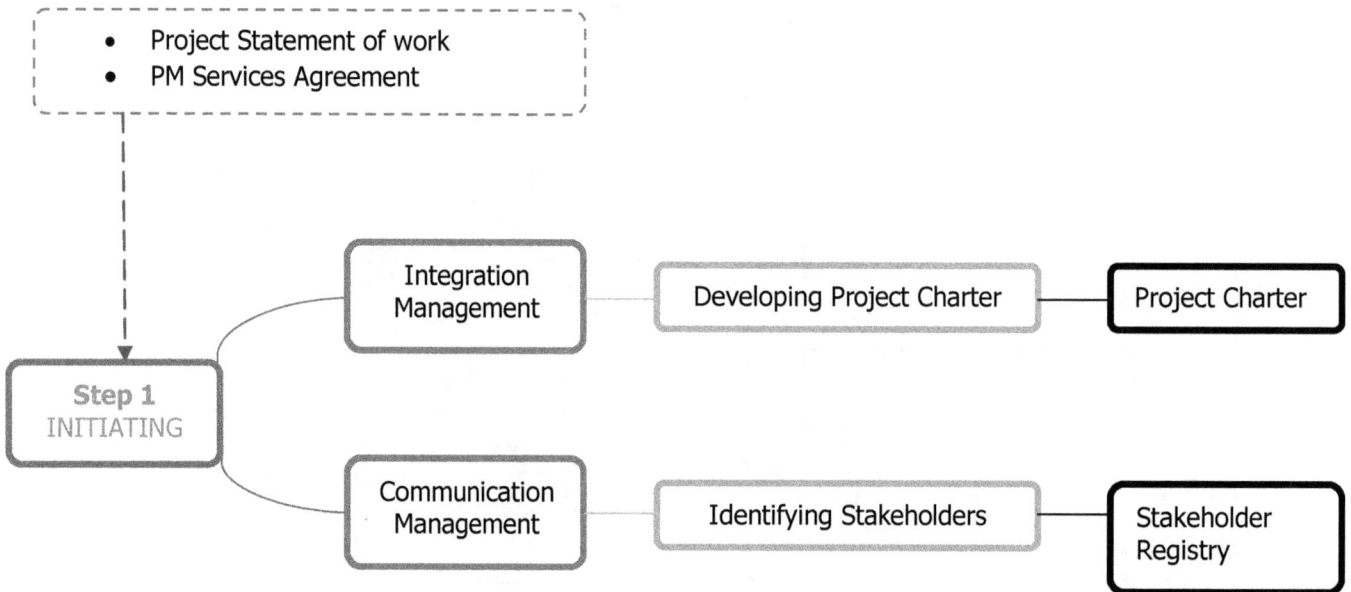

PM Services Agreement

The Contract Agreement is a legal document subject for remedy in court. It serves as a legal binding agreement between two parties: (1) the sponsor or customer, and (2) the project manager or service provider. It can also be a contract between sellers and buyers.

Hot Tip

Purchase Order, more commonly known as P.O., is a simple form of contract.

Template : Contract Agreement

Project Statement of Work

For internal projects, the Statement of Work is a document to be created by the customer or sponsor describing the scope of the entire project, services to be rendered, and needs to be delivered.

For external projects, the Statement of Work can be a part of bid documents, such as request for bid, or part of the contract from the customer. The document will serve as an initial overview of the project and an input needed in the preparation of project charter.

Hot Tip

Project Statement of Work may not be complete or comprehensive, as project details will be further defined in the project scope statement.

Template : Project Statement of Work

PROJECT CHARTER

The Project Charter recognizes and authorizes the project. It formally appoints or assigns a project manager to a specific project and defines his level of authority. It is being created in the first step of project management.

Hot Tip

In a construction project, some sponsors or customers initially hire architectural designers who will allow them to see the overall outcome of the project before getting a project manager. On the other hand, there are sponsors or customers who look for project managers just to manage the actual construction project.

This is risky. The project manager should be involved in the initial stage of the project, particularly during the design stage. When the project charter has been issued, the project manager will now get the team.

Key Point

- The project will not exist without the project charter.

- The project charter formally authorizes the project.

- This will be issued by the sponsor. However, the project manager can assist the sponsor in preparing the document.

Template : Project Charter

STAKEHOLDER REGISTRY

Provides information on the interest of the stakeholder. This document is ideally used to identify the stakeholder who can supply all the data regarding the project requirements. Generally, this document is created in the first step of project management.

Template : Stakeholder registry

Reference No. : CM-PEC-D-0001-2015

PROJECT CHARTER

1.0   PROJECT DESCRIPTION

This shows a descriptive summary of the project.

The Management of P.E.C. School have noticed the increase of college students every school year and decided to have an additional school building to accommodate the increasing number of enrollees on each offered courses. The additional school building will be constructed adjacent to building A inside the school campus. The proposed school building will consist of eight (8) floors and will included a basement and a roof deck, with an average floor area of 2,000 square meters per level.

2.0   PROJECT PURPOSE

This enumerates primary reason(s) why the project is needed.

The project aims to construct a new school building for the increasing number of students who will enroll for our existing and new courses. The new building to be constructed will include an auditorium, cafeteria, computer laboratory, case rooms, computer rooms, classrooms, offices, landscape, ramps, pathways, and other areas necessary for learning.

3.0   PROJECT JUSTIFICATION

This shows a brief explanation of the project in terms of business.

This project is to be completed before the opening of the school year 2013. We expect the increase of enrollees for our existing and new courses to be offered; it will attract new students in our region and nearby areas, and thus, will result to increase in revenue for our school by at least $600,000 for the year 2013.

4.0   PROJECT MANAGER

This enumerates the people will lead and manage the project.

Name	Organization	Contact Details	Assignment Date	Authority Level
Pier John	Pier Engineering and Consultants	Tel: Email:	April 16 , 2013	• Manage and Lead the Project • Manage and Approve Cost baseline • Manage and Approve Schedule baseline

					• Determine and Approve final Project Budget • Determine and Approve Team Members • Manage and Approve Changes

5.0 RESOURCES

This identifies who and what resources will be provided to finish the project.

Name	Role	Organization	Contact Details	Assignment Date	Remarks
Marvin Gamboa	Project Leader	Pier Engineering and Consultants	Tel: Email:	May 16 , 2013	Assigned
Name	Contractor's Leader	Company X	Tel: Email:	May 16 , 2013	Assigned
Others					To be determined by the Project Manager

6.0 STAKEHOLDERS

This identifies the group of people who will be the affected, have impact on, and benefit from the project.

Name	Role / Interest
Project Team	The team will be the responsible in delivering all necessary requirements for the successful completion of the project.
P.E.C Management	The President of P.E.C School is the sponsor of the project and should be informed about the updated project status.
Pier Engineering and Consultants Team	Pier Engineering and Consultants Team will lead the entire project until its completion.
Local Government and Authority	Local government agencies and authorities shall implement the standards and area ordinances and ensure that these will be observed throughout the project.

| Designer's Team | The designer's team are the ones responsible in ensuring that the established standards, plans, and specifications will be properly applied throughout the project. |
| Campus Faculty, Students, Groups, and Public. | The campus faculty, together with the students, organizations, and even the public, will also ensure that the established standards, regulations, and all requirements are applied throughout the execution of the project |

7.0 SCOPE

This identifies the boundaries, limitations, and range of the portion of the project.

The scope will cover the following items:

01.   Civil Works
02.   Architectural Works
03.   Site/Earth Works
04.   Concrete Works
05.   Metal Works
06.   Masonry Works
07.   Moisture and Thermal Protection
08.   Curtain Walls, Louvers, Doors, and Windows
09.   Sky Light and Canopy
10.   Finishes
11.   Plumbing Works

The items below, on the other hand, are not included in the scope initially. P.E.C School will be the one responsible in providing these items:

01.   Electrical Works

- Lighting and Power System
- Fire Alarm and Detection System
- Auxiliaries
    o Electronic Safety and Security Works
    o Audio / Video System
    o Public Address (P.A. System)
    o Structured Cabling Works
    o Telephone Wiring System
- Supply and Installation of Electric Generating Set
- Lightning Protection System

02.   Mechanical Works
- Heat ,Ventilation and Air conditioning System (HVAC)
- Supply and Installation Elevator Equipment
03.   Supply of Lighting Fixtures

04.   Supply of Plumbing Fixtures
05.   Supply of Pumps and Pump Controllers
06.   Supply of Air conditioning Equipment
07.   Supply Floor / Wall Tiles and Carpets
08.   Supply and Installation Operable Wall System
09.   Supply Furniture /Chairs / Loose Cabinet / Glass Whiteboard
10.   Supply of Fire Extinguishers
11.   Supply of Signage and Directories
12.   Supply Sewage Treatment Plant
13.   Supply of Dry Type Transformer For Elevator (when necessary)
14.   Supply Fans / Blowers and Exhaust Fans.

8.0 DELIVERABLES

This specifies the expected results of the project.

Categories	Description
Building Structure	A complete and fully-furnished eight-storey building as part of the P.E.C School, including the roof deck for auditorium use and the basement as canteen and offices
Services	Functional and operational supply of electricity, water, lightings, air conditioning, telephone lines, internet, fans and blowers, sewage treatment, drainage, fire alarm and detection, lightning protection and elevators
Building Access	Ramps, pathways, and stairs
Facilities	Complete, fully-furnished, and functional classrooms, case rooms, faculty rooms, computer laboratory rooms, offices, auditorium, canteen, and coffee shop.

9.0 CONSTRAINTS

This specifies the established limits and/or restrictions of the project

01.   The new P.E.C. School Building will be finished on or before April 16, 2014.
02.   The allotted budget for the project is $10,000,000.
03.   The allowed time for concrete pouring is from 6:00 PM to 7:00 AM only, when classes are not being held in the school property.
04.   The delivery of project materials inside the school vicinity from 6:00 PM to 7:00 AM only.
05.   The project site will maintain the "no noise and no dust" policy.

10.0 ASSUMPTION

These are additional statements related to the project that are believed to be true even without proof.

- The Design and Technical Team will be available on site to assist the project activity.
- All the required resources and services are available in the area and nearby provinces.

Approval:

Pier Engineering and Consultants   **P.E.C School**

By: By:

_____   _____   _____

Pier John   **Alexander Thomas**   **Richard Ramos**

Project Manager   Vice President   President

Company Address :
Telephone :
Fax :
Email : info@
Website : www.

Template ID: IT-COM-001
Date Prepared : 02/28/15
Revision : 000
Pages : 1 of 1
Reference No. : CM-PEC-D-0002-2015

Your Logo here!

Stakeholder Registry

Project	Name of the Project
Project Package	Name of the package / phase of the project
Project Location	Name of the location of the project

Name	Position (Company)	Role (Project)	Contact Details	Requirements	Expectation	Influence	Category	Analysis					
								Power		Interest		Impact Assessment	Possible Strategies (to gain support / minimizing hindrance)
								Low (A)	High (B)	Low (C)	High (D)		
Pier John	Senior Engineer	Project Manager	Mobile: Tel email				Internal/ External/resistor/ supporters etc.						

When :
B-C (keep contented)
B-D (Manage carefully)
A-C (Monitor)
A-D (continuously Informed)

PROJECT STATEMENT OF WORK

1.0 PROJECT DESCRIPTION

This provides a descriptive summary of the project.

The proposed school building will have eight (8) floors, including basement and roof deck, and will measure an average floor area of 2,000 square meters per level or floor. The said building will be constructed inside the school campus and will include facilities such as coffee shop, canteen, computer laboratory, case rooms, computer rooms, classrooms, offices, landscape, ramps, pathways, and an auditorium.

The primary purpose of this project is to accommodate new enrollees for the existing and new courses being offered in the school.

2.0 PROJECT SCOPE DESCRIPTION

- Civil Works
- Architectural Works
- Site/Earth Works
- Concrete Works
- Metal Works
- Masonry Works
- Moisture and Thermal Protection
- Curtain Walls, Louvers, Doors, and Windows
- Sky Light and Canopy
- Finishes
- Plumbing Works
-

Not covered in the scope:

- Electrical Works

    Lighting and Power System
    Fire Alarm and Detection System
    Auxiliaries
    Supply and Installation of Electric Generating Set
    Lightning Protection System

- Mechanical Works

    Heat, Ventilation and Air conditioning System (HVAC)
    Supply and Installation Elevator Equipment

- Supply of Lighting Fixtures
- Supply of Plumbing Fixtures
- Supply of Pumps and Pump Controllers
- Supply of Air conditioning Equipment
- Supply Floor / Wall Tiles and Carpets
- Supply and Installation Operable Wall System
- Supply Furniture /Chairs / Loose Cabinet / Glass Whiteboard
- Supply of Fire Extinguishers
- Supply of Signage and Directories
- Supply Sewage Treatment Plant
- Supply of Dry Type Transformer For Elevator (when necessary)
- Supply Fans / Blowers and Exhaust Fans.

Prepared by: _____

P.E.C School

_____   _____

Alexander Thomas   **Richard Ramos**

Vice President   President

PROJECT MANAGEMENT (PM)
SERVICES AGREEMENT

BELOW ARE THE COMPONENTS OF THE PROJECT MANAGEMENT CONTRACT BUT NOT LIMITED TO; *(Please refer to your legal advisor)*

1. ARTICLE I
   - DEFINITION OF TERMS
2. ARTICLE II
   - THE SERVICES
3. ARTICLE III
   - OBLIGATIONS OF THE OWNER
4. ARTICLE IV
   - PERSONNEL
5. ARTICLE V
   - CONTRACT AMOUNT AND METHOD OF PAYMENT
6. ARTICLE VI
   - INDEMNITY
7. ARTICLE VII
   - FORCE MAJEURE AND OTHER CAUSES
8. ARTICLE VIII
   - MODIFICATION
9. ARTICLE IX
   - TERMINATION OF SERVICES
10. ARTICLE X
    - LIABILITY OF THE CONSULTANT
11. ARTICLE XI
    - DISPUTE AND ARBITRATION
12. ARTICLE XII
    - OWNERSHIP OF STUDIES, DATA AND PLANS
13. ARTICLE XIII
    - COMMENCEMENT AND DURATION OF CONTRACT
14. ARTICLE XIV

Step 2

Planning

STEP 2 :   PLANNING

Planning is the second step in managing projects. It is composed of process groups aimed to establish a concrete project management plan and identify all the necessary documents for the project. These process groups enable the stakeholders and project managers to create a comprehensive and detailed scope, schedule, costing, and other required information that will help them manage and control established plans for the project.

Flow Chart : Project Management process is not always sequential or performed in identical

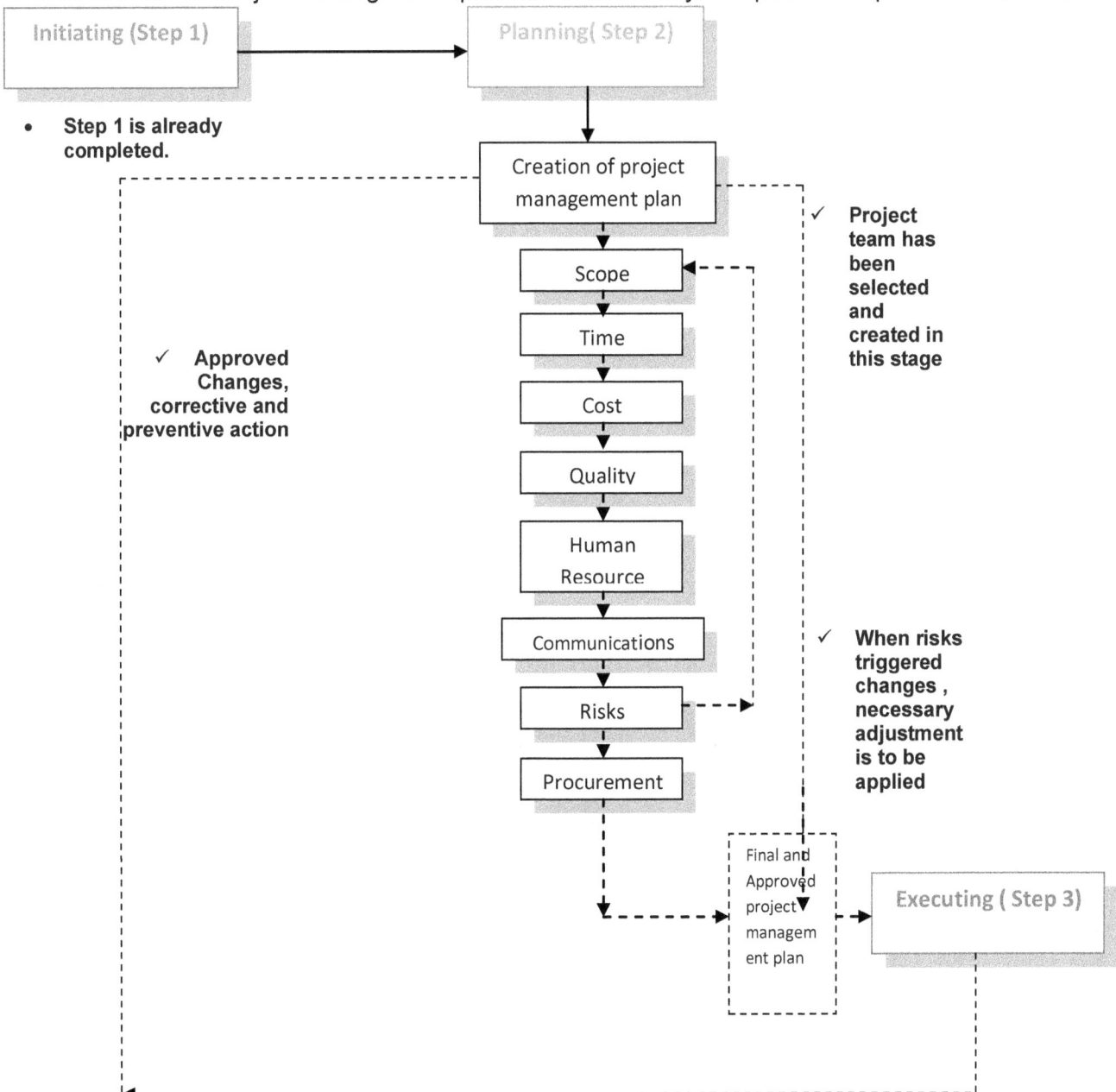

Initiating (Step 1)	Planning(Step 2)

- **Step 1 is already completed.**

Creation of project management plan

✓ **Project team has been selected and created in this stage**

Scope

Time

✓ **Approved Changes, corrective and preventive action**

Cost

Quality

Human Resource

Communications

✓ **When risks triggered changes , necessary adjustment is to be applied**

Risks

Procurement

Final and Approved project management plan

Executing (Step 3)

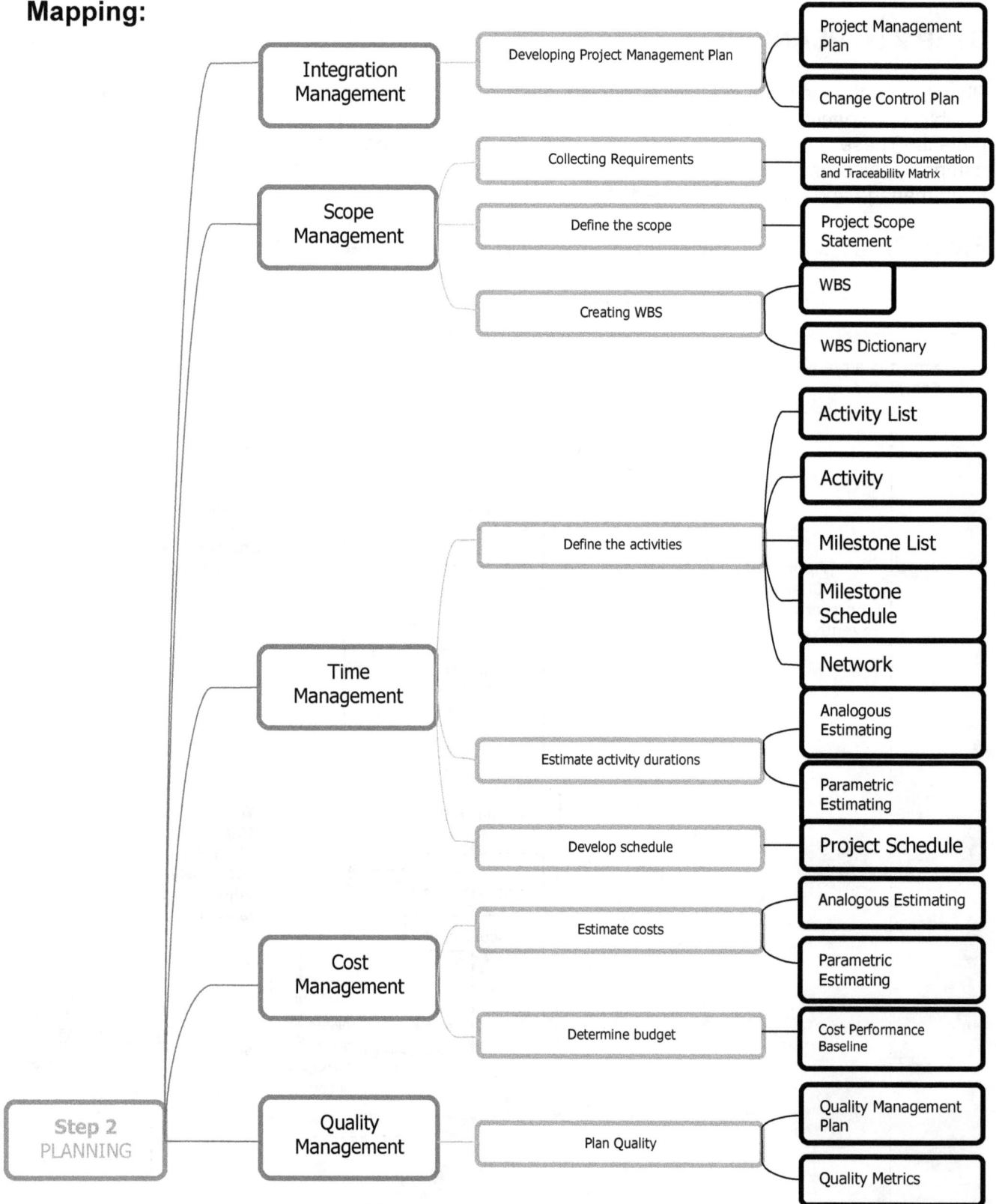

Mapping:

```
Step 2
PLANNING
    │
    ├── Integration Management ── Developing Project Management Plan ──┬── Project Management Plan
    │                                                                  └── Change Control Plan
    │
    ├── Scope Management ──┬── Collecting Requirements ── Requirements Documentation and Traceability Matrix
    │                      ├── Define the scope ── Project Scope Statement
    │                      └── Creating WBS ──┬── WBS
    │                                         └── WBS Dictionary
    │
    ├── Time Management ──┬── Define the activities ──┬── Activity List
    │                     │                           ├── Activity
    │                     │                           ├── Milestone List
    │                     │                           ├── Milestone Schedule
    │                     │                           └── Network
    │                     ├── Estimate activity durations ──┬── Analogous Estimating
    │                     │                                 └── Parametric Estimating
    │                     └── Develop schedule ── Project Schedule
    │
    ├── Cost Management ──┬── Estimate costs ──┬── Analogous Estimating
    │                     │                    └── Parametric Estimating
    │                     └── Determine budget ── Cost Performance Baseline
    │
    └── Quality Management ── Plan Quality ──┬── Quality Management Plan
                                            └── Quality Metrics
```

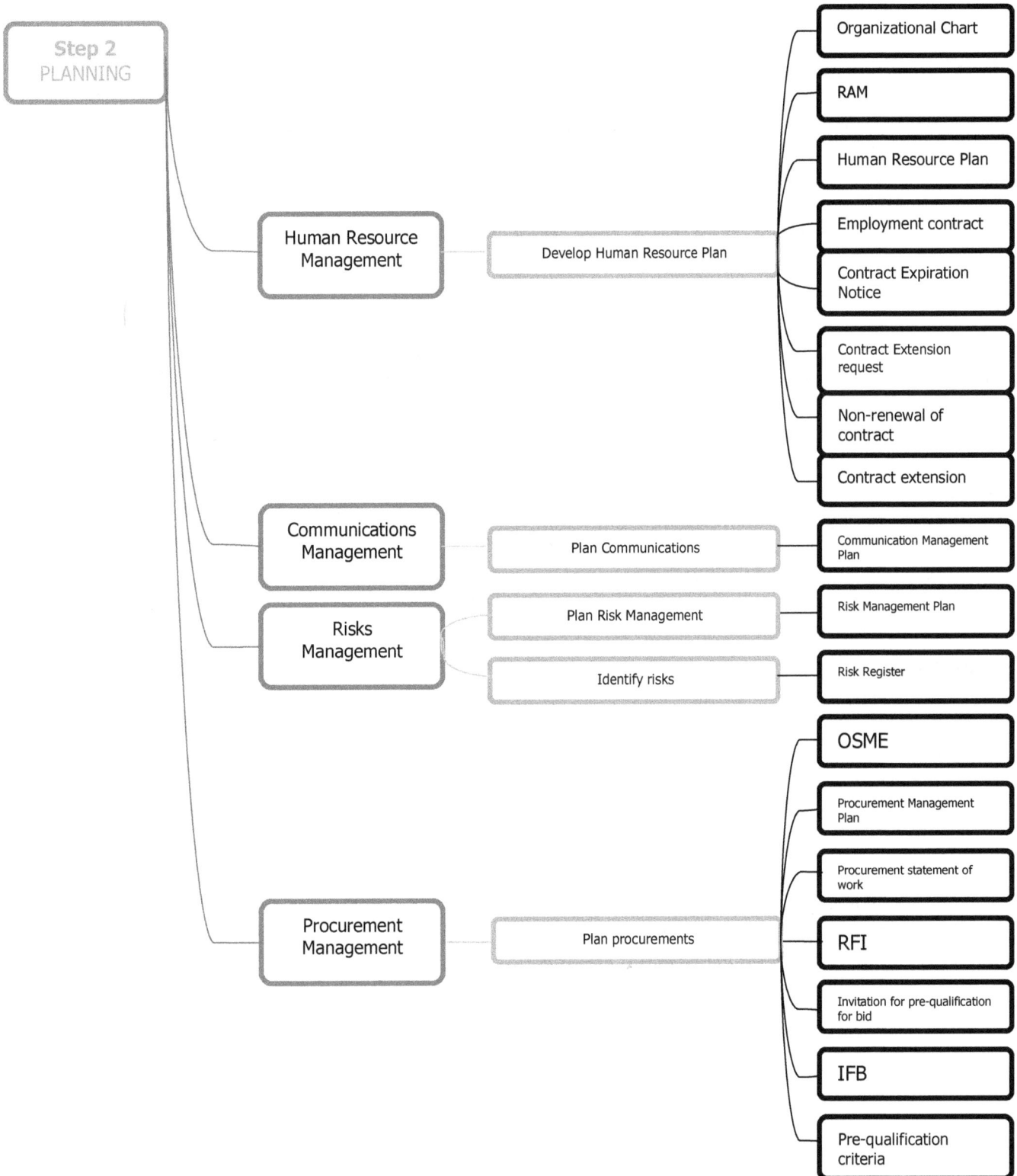

Step 2
PLANNING

Human Resource Management — Develop Human Resource Plan
- Organizational Chart
- RAM
- Human Resource Plan
- Employment contract
- Contract Expiration Notice
- Contract Extension request
- Non-renewal of contract
- Contract extension

Communications Management — Plan Communications
- Communication Management Plan

Risks Management
- Plan Risk Management — Risk Management Plan
- Identify risks — Risk Register

Procurement Management — Plan procurements
- OSME
- Procurement Management Plan
- Procurement statement of work
- RFI
- Invitation for pre-qualification for bid
- IFB
- Pre-qualification criteria

PROJECT MANAGEMENT PLAN

Is an approved plan that describes how the project will be executed, monitored, controlled, communicated, and closed out. This document follows a specific type of format either summary type or a more detailed outline. It also includes some subsidiary management plans listed below.

Template : Project Management Plan

CHANGE CONTROL PLAN

Is a vital part of the project management plan, which consists of the processes of analyzing, evaluating, approving, and managing changes to project document, deliverables, and the project management plan itself. It is often being done from the start to completion of the project.

Template : Change Control Plan

REQUIREMENTS DOCUMENTATION AND TRACEABILITY MATRIX

Requirements documentation is a list of all requirements associated with the project and can be categorize as stakeholder and priority, or trade and technical. Lists of requirements will be progressively elaborated as the data becomes available on the project. This document is usually created during the second step of managing projects.

Also included in this form is the Requirements Traceability Matrix which is used to track the given requirement, link to a project purpose, and verify the identified requirements.

Template : Requirements Documentation and Traceability Matrix

Hot Tip

Document the sponsor's or customer's requirements in terms of the material supply or specific trade that they can provide. This must be noted in the early stage of planning, which is often called Owner Supplied Materials (OSM) because some owners or sponsors have their related businesses in the material and equipment supplies.

When customers or sponsors have their repeated projects like warehouses or shopping malls, they prefer to select some materials or equipment that they can use for their next project. They can remove the items with mark ups (upcoming contractor), so that they can save money from it.

PROJECT SCOPE STATEMENT

Is where the project deliverables are described in details and the necessary requirements, including expected work and output, are elaborated .This serves as an important guide for the execution of the project by the team members and provide the team with the detailed planning approach.

Furthermore, project scope statement provides in-depth information for change request as additive or deductive. This document is often created during the second step of managing projects.

Template : Project Scope Statement

Work Breakdown Structure(WBS)

Is where the project will be broken down into smaller manageable pieces. It is designed to be in a top-down decomposition of the project with the lowest level as the work package. The representation of work breakdown structure involves a hierarchical chart format and breakdown lists format. This document is generally created during the second step of managing projects.

Key Point

- The top level is the project title.

- The project must be broken down into smaller and manageable pieces, all the way up to work package level. There is no rule of thumb in breaking down the project into WBS. It can be outsourced or contracted, can be estimated, cannot be logically divided, and deliverables are to be defined.

- Provide numbering for easy identification and further use, such as cost coding.

- WBS should be created with the help of the team.

Template : WBS

WBS DICTIONARY

Work breakdown structure dictionary provides supplemental details to WBS, such as detailed description of work to be done, detailed information of work packages, and control accounts for cost. This document is often created during the second step of managing projects.

Template : WBS Dictionary

Hot Tip

- Work not included in the WBS is not part of the project.
- You cannot finish a successful project without WBS. This is the foundation of any project.
- With every project you have, document the WBS and use the previous one as template for future similar projects.

23

ACTIVITY LIST AND ATTRIBUTES

Is a list of all activities associated with the work packages to complete the project. The work package from our WBS is to be decomposed further in to activity level, where it can easily managed, monitored, and estimated. Our lists of activity will then be arranged and sequenced for the next process.

Together with the form is the Activity Attributes. We establish the more detailed description of an activity by specifying the resources needed for this activity assumption and constraints and predecessor and successor activity.

These documents are to be created during the second step of managing projects.

Templates : Activity List
Activity Attributes

MILESTONE LIST

Specifies the relative time or event for the project. The document comprises all the milestones – whether optional, mandatory, or based on historical data and information. This document is often created during the second step of managing projects.

Template : Milestone list

NETWORK DIAGRAM

Is a type of diagram where activities involved in the project are to be arranged and sequenced according to how the entire work will be performed as a whole group of activities. It shows the dependencies of activities using critical path or time scaled diagram. This document is created during the second step of managing projects.

There are two (2) ways on how to draw network diagram. First is the Precedence Diagramming Method (PDM) and the second one is the Arrow Diagramming Method (ADM). The PDM or Activity-on-Node (AON) involves boxes or nodes that represent activities connected by arrow that symbolize their dependencies. On the other hand, ADM or Activity-on-Arrow (AOA), involves arrows that represent activities and boxes that symbolize dependencies. This type of diagram usually has finish-to-start relationships and may use dummies for activities.

Template : Network Diagram

ACTIVITY DURATION ESTIMATES

Refers to the estimated working period that will take to finish the established activity. Duration estimates can be performed by using analogous estimating, parametric estimating, or three-point estimating. This document is usually created during the second step of managing projects.

Template : Analogous Estimating
Parametric Estimating

PROJECT SCHEDULE

Is a representation of a desired format where the activities of the project show the starting date, end date, completed activities, milestones, and relationships. It can be presented in various formats, including tabular, bar charts, Gantt charts, milestone charts, or schedule network diagrams. This document is often created during the second step of managing projects.

- Unrealistic schedule is project manager's fault!

Hot Tip

Template : Project Schedule

ACTIVITY COST ESTIMATES

Is the application of measurable method to establish costs of the resources needed to complete the activity. Cost estimates are often expressed in currency units, such as dollar and peso, and will be progressively elaborated and refined when data and information are available.

Generally, cost of an activity refers to costs pertaining to materials, manpower or labor, equipment, services, and contingencies. Activity cost estimates can be performed by using analogous estimating, parametric estimating, three-point estimating, or bottom-up estimating.

This document is to be created during the second step of managing projects.
Templates: Analogous Estimating
Parametric Estimating

COST PERFORMANCE BASELINE

Is a time phased budget at completion of the project. This is commonly presented in the form of S-Curve for monitoring and controlling the cost for the project. This document is often created during the second step of managing projects.
Templates: S-Curve

QUALITY MANAGEMENT PLAN

Is part of or a subsidiary plan of the project management plan. This plan includes establishing methods, processes, and procedures to be able to meet the defined requirements of the project. It is important to establish what the acceptable deliverables are, what to do to meet the requirements of being acceptable, and how it will be measured against the requirements. This document is being created during the second step of managing projects.

Hot Tip

- For team members, always check the quality by self-inspection. The entire organization has responsibilities in terms of quality.

- Poor quality of the project is project manager's fault!

- Spend more time in improving the quality and processes.

- Spend more time and money in quality concerns..

Template: Quality Management Plan

QUALITY METRICS

Includes the exact values that are to be measured on a certain project. This includes the acceptable measurement, including limits and controls in terms of specific values. The values in the metrics are to be measured during the quality control process , and knowing the limits from the metrics will result to acceptable deliverables and corrective or preventive actions. This document is being created during the second step of managing projects.

understanding of their respective roles and responsibilities. It also serves as a graphic representation of relationships and positions in a top-down format. This document is being created during the second step of managing projects.

Hot Tip

You can also check approved drawing plans, architectural, structural, and all required trades. All measurements, including vertical height, horizontal, thickness, inclined, elevations, diameters, and gauges, are parts of quality metrics with direct measurement approach. It is good to bring the drawing on site and measure actual sizes as per approved drawing plan (signed and marked with FOR CONSTRUCTION). Other bring smaller printed version (like A3 size) on site for convenience with blow up details. *(See sample template)*

Tests like compressive strength of concrete and tensile for reinforcing steel can be conducted. However, take note that when testing is being done, be sure to have an inspector or technical consultant with you to check and verify the calibration of the testing apparatus or equipment being used. *(See sample template)*

Hot Tip

- Create and post organizational chart inside the office. You can create one per team or per group, so that contractors, for example, have their own chart in their office.
- You can also post an organizational chart in the conference room, and include basic contact and picture of the whole team with their key persons like contractor, project management team, and other consultants for quick reference.

Templates: Organizational Chart

RESPONSIBILITY ASSIGN MATRIX (RAM)

Responsibility Assign Matrix or RAM is a document that shows the relations between work packages or project activities and the project team. Through this document, all the tasks and activities concerning a specific person or team can be defined and established, serving as a comprehensive guide to each team members involved in the project. RAM uses the RACI method – Responsible, Accountable, Consult, and Inform. This document is being created during the second step of managing projects.

Template: RAM

Templates: Quality Metrics

ORGANIZATIONAL CHART

Is a document that highlights the role and responsibility of the team and each person comprising it. The chart also features each work package under work breakdown structure that has a definite owner and clear

HUMAN RESOURCE PLAN

Is an essential component of the project management plan that creates a system on how the human resources will be staffed, managed, and released. This document is being created during the second step of managing projects.

Templates: Human Resource Plan
, Employment Contract, Contract Expiration Notice, Contract Extension Request, Non-Renewal of Contract, Contract Extension

COMMUNICATION MANAGEMENT PLAN

Is another essential component of the project management plan. It involves a system on how to address information for stakeholder that answers what form of communication, when, and how frequent should it be done .This document is often created during the second step of managing projects.

Template: Communication Management Plan

RISK MANAGEMENT PLAN

Is another essential component of the project management plan, designed to deal with possible risks of the project and preventing issues that may result to negative or bad effect. In return, it specifies steps on how to come up with positive results or good effects by establishing plans in the first place before any problems might occur. This document is to be created during the second step of managing projects.

Template: Risk Management Plan

RISK REGISTER

Is a list of identified risks that may occur during the project execution. The list can be identified by using some tools and techniques, including checklist analysis that evaluates risks from the lowest level of risk breakdown structure to the highest. This document is usually created during the second step of managing projects.

Template: Risk Register

PROCUREMENT MANAGEMENT PLAN

Is another essential component of project management plan that addresses the procurement process, including documentation, managing, and closure of contracts. This document is often created during the second step of managing projects.

Templates: Procurement Management Plan , Owner Supplied Materials and Equipment (OSME) - *you can this templates for construction project.*

PROCUREMENT STATEMENT OF WORK

Is a document that can be developed from the project scope. It comes from a portion of the project scope to be considered for contracting packages. This should include detailed information such as location of work, quantity, specification, specified quality, and work schedule. This document is often created during the second step of managing projects.

Template: Procurement Statement of Work

PROCUREMENT DOCUMENTS

Are written materials that ask for proposals from prospective sellers. There are different types of procurement documents, including request for information (RFI), request for proposal (RFP), request for quotation (RFQ), invitation for bid (IFB), and tender notice. This document is often created during the second step of managing projects.

Templates: Request For Information (RFI), Invitation For Prequalification, Invitation For Bid (IFB)

SOURCE SELECTION CRITERIA

Is a type of document that is often included in the procurement documents. We establish criteria to rate the sellers' proposals in terms of points or score. Selection criteria may be broad or simple, depending on the extent of the project. Criteria are usually based on financial proposals and technical proposals.

This document is being created during the second step of managing projects.

Template: Prequalification Criteria

Project Management Plan		**Date Prepared :** 02/28/15	**Template ID:** PT-P-001
Project	Name of the Project	**Revision :** 000	**Pages :** 1 of 1
Project Package	Name of the package / phase of the project		
Project Location	Name of the location of the project	**Reference No. :** CM-PEC-D-0004-2015	

Project Management Plan Composition

Plans

Scope management plan
Cost management plan
Schedule management plan
Quality management plan
Communications management plan
Procurement management plan
Risk management plan
Human resource plan
Integrated change control plan
  ➢ Change control plan

Baselines

Scope baseline
Schedule baseline
Cost baseline
Quality baseline

Change Control Plan		Date Prepared : 02/28/15	Template ID: PT-P-002
Project	Name of the Project	**Revision :** 000	**Pages :** 1 of 1
Project Package	Name of the package / phase of the project		
Project Location	Name of the location of the project	**Reference No. :** CM-PEC-D-0005-2015	

Change Control Board:

Name	Role	Responsibility	Organization	Authority Level

Changes:

Baseline	Description	Impact
Scope		
Schedule		
Cost		
Quality		

Process: *(Establish the process you used or create a process flow you adopted.*

Your Logo here!

Requirements Documentation and Traceability

		Date Prepared : 02/28/15	Template ID: PT-SC-001
Project	Name of the Project	**Revision :** 000	**Pages :** 1 of 1
Project Package	Name of the package / phase of the project		
Project Location	Name of the location of the project	**Reference No. :** CM-PEC-D-0005-2015	

ID	Category	Project Requirements Description	Stakeholder	Priority	Impact / connects to Project Purpose	Source	Test / Verification	Acceptance Criteria	Approval	Status

Company Address :
Telephone :
Fax :
Email : info@
Website : www.

Project Scope Statement

		Date Prepared : 02/28/15	Template ID: PT-SC-002
Project	Name of the Project	**Revision :** 000	**Pages :** 1 of 1
Project Package	Name of the package / phase of the project		
Project Location	Name of the location of the project	**Reference No. :** CM-PEC-D-0007-2015	

SCOPE

ID	Category	Description

Deliverables

ID	Category	Description	Acceptance Criteria

Project Milestone:

Project Schedule:

Exclusion:

Assumption:

	Company Address :
Your Logo here!	Email : info@
	Website : www.

Work Breakdown Structure(WBS)		Date Prepared : 02/28/15	Template ID: PT-SC-003
Project	Name of the Project	**Revision :** 000	**Pages :** 1 of 1
Project Package	Name of the package / phase of the project		
Project Location	Name of the location of the project	**Reference No. :** CM-PEC-D-0008-2015	

HIERARCHICAL CHART FORMAT

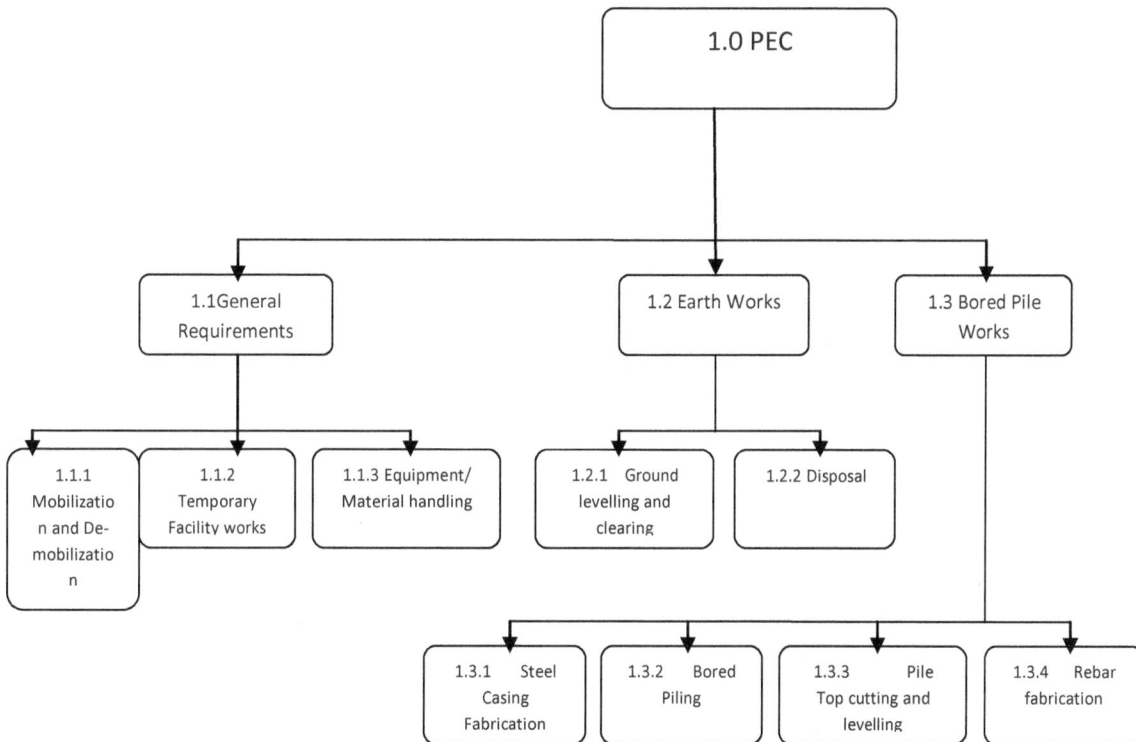

Your Logo here!

WBS Dictionary

		Date Prepared : 02/28/15	Template ID: PT-SC-004
Project	Name of the Project	**Revision :** 000	**Pages :** 1 of 2
Project Package	Name of the package / phase of the project		
Project Location	Name of the location of the project	**Reference No. :** CM-PEC-D-0009-2015	

Work Package ID	Work Package Description	Control Account ID	Responsible (Team /Group / Individual)
Quality Requirements	Acceptance Criteria	Technical References	Status
Duration		Milestones 1. 2.	
Interdependencies	Before This Work Package : After This Work Package :	Due Date :	

Your Logo here!

WBS Dictionary

Date Issue :	Pages :
02/28/15	2 of 2
Reference No. : CM-PEC-D-0009-2015	
Revision No. : 000	

Cost Estimates :

ID	Activity Description	Unit	Quantity	Unit Rate				Total Amount	Resources
				Materials	Labor	Others	Total		

Approved by : Signature:

Project Manager's Name , Date Signed

	Company Address :
	Telephone :
	Fax :
	Email : info@
	Website : www.

Activity List			**Date Prepared :** 02/28/15	**Template ID:** PT-T-001
Project	Name of the Project		**Revision :** 000	**Pages :** 1 of 1
Project Package	Name of the package / phase of the project			
Project Location	Name of the location of the project		**Reference No. :** CM-PEC-D-0010-2015	

ID	WBS	Work Package	Activity	Description
1.1.2	General Requirements	Temporary Facility Works	Lay outing and Survey	
			Footing excavation	
			Installation of Pedestal	
			Installation of Steel Containers (as built in office)	
			Ceiling works	
			Installation of insulation for walls and ceiling	

Activity Attributes

		Date Prepared : 02/28/15	Template ID: PT-T-002
Project	Name of the Project	Revision : 000	Pages : 1 of 1
Project Package	Name of the package / phase of the project		
Project Location	Name of the location of the project	Reference No.: CM-PEC-D-0011-2015	

WBS : *(Name and ID of the WBS)*   **Work Package :** *(Name and ID of the work)*   **Date Prepared :**

ID	Activity	Description	Predecessor Activity :	Successor Activity :	Constraints (date)
			Logical Relationships	Logical Relationships	**Assumption :**
			Leads / Lags	Leads / Lags	**Where to Make this Activity :**

Resource Requirements

Materials		Equipment		People	
Quantity	Description	Quantity	Description	Quantity	Description

Responsible for This Activity

Name :	Location:

Company Address :
Telephone :
Fax :
Email : info@
Website : www.

Milestone List

		Date Prepared: 02/28/15	Template ID: PT-T-003
Project	Name of the Project	**Revision :** 000	**Pages :** 1 of 1
Project Package	Name of the package / phase of the project		
Project Location	Name of the location of the project	**Reference No. :** CM-PEC-D-0012-2015	

ID	Description of Activity	Milestone	
		Started	**Finished**
1.1 S	General Requirements - Started	May 01, 2013	
1.1.1	Mobilization		May 14,2013
1.1.2	Temporary Facilities Installation/erection		June 21,2013
1.1.3	Material Handling and logistics		June 21,2013
1.1.4	Demobilization		June 28,2013
1.1 F	General Requirements - Finished		June 28,2013
1.2 S	Earth Works- Started	May 03,2013	
1.2.1	Clearing, grabbing and trimming		May 21,2013
1.2.2	Hauling and disposal of excavated and cleared materials		May 21,2013
1.2 F	Earth Works- Finished		June 28,2013
1.3 S	Load Bearing Elements and Foundation -Started	May 03,2013	
1.3.1	Steel Casing Fabrication		May 21,2013
1.3.2	Bored Pile installation and Activities		June 21,2013
1.3.3	Top of Piles trimming		June 21,2013
1.3.4	Rebar Case fabrication		June 14,2013
1.3.5	Survey and Lay-out		June 14,2013
1.3 F	Load Bearing Elements and Foundation -Finished		June 21,2013

This Milestone lists is for illustrative only and not intended to portray any projects, scope and description or not representing any specific ways to organize, plan of any type of projects.

Milestone Schedule

Template ID:	PT-T-004
Date Prepared : 02/28/15	
Revision : 000	Pages : 1 of 1
Reference No. : CM-PEC-D-0013-2015	

Project	P.E.C School Building
Project Package	Bored Piling Works
Project Location	Name of the location of the project

WBS ID	Description of Activity	Schedule May	Schedule June
1.1	General Requirements - Started	05/01	
1.1.1	Mobilization - Completed	05/14	
1.1.2	Temporary Facilities Installation/erection - Completed		06/21
1.1.3	Material Handling and logistics - Completed		06/21
1.2.1	Clearing ,grabbing and levelling - Completed	05/21	
1.2.2	Hauling and disposal - Completed	05/21	
1.3	Load Bearing Elements and Foundation -Finished		
1.4	Finished		06/28

This Milestone Schedule is for illustrative only and not intended to portray any construction projects , scope ,description or not representing any specific ways to organize , plan of any type of construction projects.

Network Diagram

Company Address :
Telephone :
Fax :
Email : info@
Website.: www.

Date Prepared : 02/28/15	Template ID: PT-T-005
Revision : 000	Pages : 1 of 1
Reference No.:	CM-PEC-D-0014-2015

Project	Name of the Project
Project Package	Name of the package / phase of the project
Project Location	Name of the location of the project

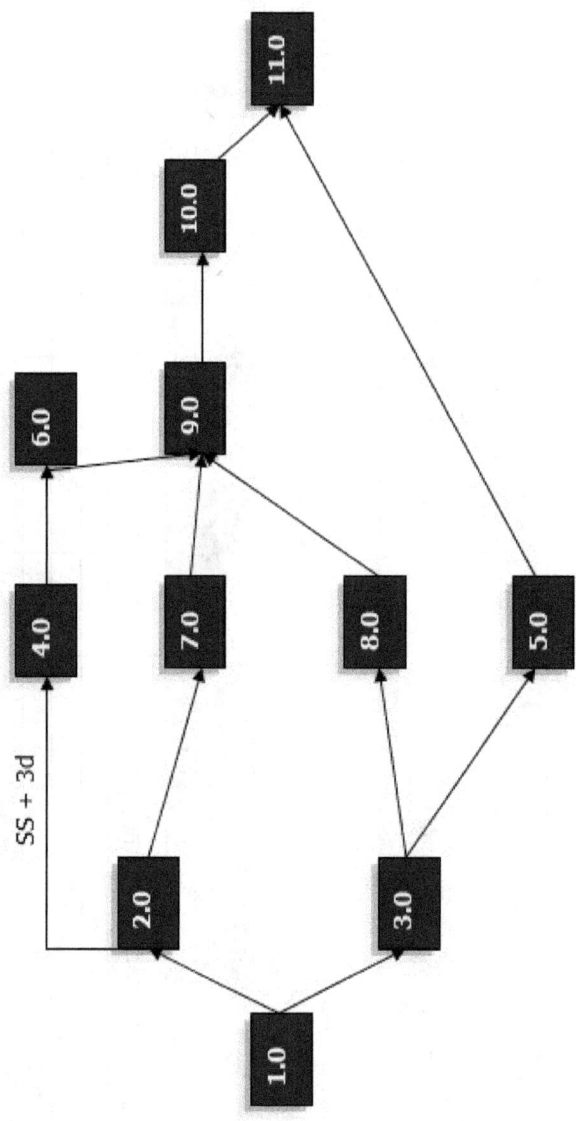

ID	Activity Description
1.0	Start
2.0	Mobilization
3.0	Temporary Facilities Installations
4.0	Clearing
5.0	Survey and Lay out
6.0	Fabrication of Steel casing
7.0	Hauling/Disposal of Cleared/excavated Material
8.0	Fabrication of Rebars
9.0	Bored Piling Works
10.0	Demobilization
11.0	End

This illustration , List is for illustrative only and not intended to portray any construction projects , scope ,description or not representing any specific ways to organize , plan of any type of construction projects.

Analogous Estimating - Time

		Date Prepared: 02/28/15	**Template ID:** PT-T-006
Project	Name of the Project	**Revision :** 000	**Pages :** 1 of 1
Project Package	Name of the package / phase of the project		
Project Location	Name of the location of the project	**Reference No. :** CM-PEC-D-0015-2015	

WBS ID	Activity Description	Previous		Present	
		Material Quantity (A)	Duration (B)	Material Quantity (C)	Duration Estimates (B) x (C) / (A)
	Concreting of Floor Slab	10cum.			

Your Logo here!

Parametric Estimating - Time

		Date Prepared : 02/28/15	Template ID: PT-T-007
Project	Name of the Project	**Revision :** 000	**Pages :** 1 of 1
Project Package	Name of the package / phase of the project		
Project Location	Name of the location of the project	**Reference No. :** CM-PEC-D-0016-2015	

WBS ID	Activity Description	Material Quantity (A)		Productivity rate (Unit per Time) (B)	Duration Estimates(Time) (A) / (B)
		Quantity	Unit		
	Tiles installation	10	sq m	9 sqm/hr	1.11 hours

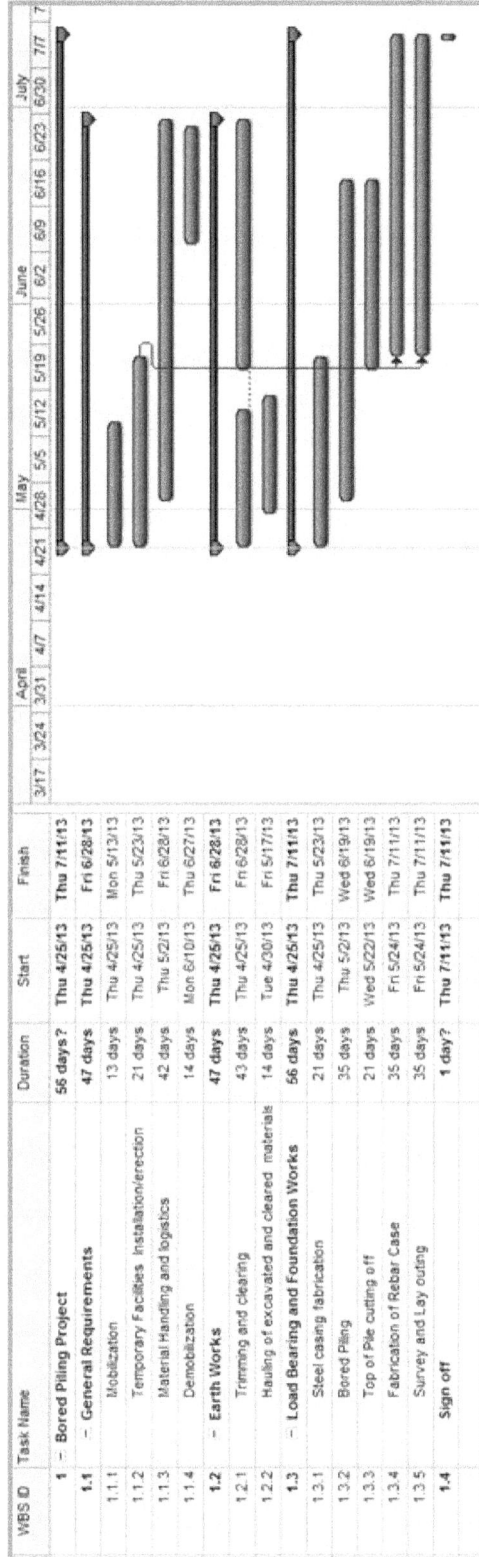

Project Schedule

Company Address :
Telephone :
Fax :
Email : info@
Website : www.

		Date Prepared : 02/28/15	Template ID: PT-T-008
Project	Name of the Project	Revision : 000	Pages : 1 of 1
Project Package	Name of the package / phase of the project		
Project Location	Name of the location of the project	Reference No.: CM-PEC-D-0017-2015	

WBS ID	Task Name	Duration	Start	Finish
1	– Bored Piling Project	56 days?	Thu 4/25/13	Thu 7/11/13
1.1	– General Requirements	47 days	Thu 4/25/13	Fri 6/28/13
1.1.1	Mobilization	13 days	Thu 4/25/13	Mon 5/13/13
1.1.2	Temporary Facilities Installation/erection	21 days	Thu 4/25/13	Thu 5/23/13
1.1.3	Material Handling and logistics	42 days	Thu 5/2/13	Fri 6/28/13
1.1.4	Demobilization	14 days	Mon 6/10/13	Thu 6/27/13
1.2	– Earth Works	47 days	Thu 4/25/13	Fri 6/28/13
1.2.1	Trimming and clearing	43 days	Thu 4/25/13	Fri 6/28/13
1.2.2	Hauling of excavated and cleared materials	14 days	Tue 4/30/13	Fri 5/17/13
1.3	– Load Bearing and Foundation Works	56 days	Thu 4/25/13	Thu 7/11/13
1.3.1	Steel casing fabrication	21 days	Thu 4/25/13	Thu 5/23/13
1.3.2	Bored Piling	35 days	Thu 5/2/13	Wed 6/19/13
1.3.3	Top of Pile cutting off	21 days	Wed 5/22/13	Wed 6/19/13
1.3.4	Fabrication of Rebar Case	35 days	Fri 5/24/13	Thu 7/11/13
1.3.5	Survey and Lay outing	35 days	Fri 5/24/13	Thu 7/11/13
1.4	Sign off	1 day?	Thu 7/11/13	Thu 7/11/13

This illustration is for illustrative only and not intended to portray any construction projects , scope , description of any type of construction projects .

Analogous Estimating - Cost

Date Prepared : 02/28/15		**Template ID:** PT-C-001	
Project	Name of the Project	**Revision :** 000	**Pages :** 1 of 1
Project Package	Name of the package / phase of the project		
Project Location	Name of the location of the project	**Reference No. :** CM-PEC-D-0018-2015	

WBS ID	Activity Description	Unit	Quantity (A)	Unit Rate(Amount / Unit) (example; $ /cum)				Amount ($ or any unit currencies)
				Material	Labor	Others (contingency)	Total	
				(B)	(C)	(D)	(E) B+C+D	(A) x (E)
	Concreting of Floor Slab	cu.m.	10					

The tabulation above is based on the assumption of the following;

- Unit Rate
  - ➤ Derived from previous similar projects
  - ➤ Is the value of Amount ($, peso, euro)per unit (cubic meter, linear meter, square foot etc.)
  - ➤ Expressed in$ / linear meter, euro /square foot etc.

Parametric Estimating - Cost

Date Prepared : 02/28/15	**Template ID:** PT-C-002

		Revision :	**Pages :**
Project	Name of the Project	000	1 of 1
Project Package	Name of the package / phase of the project		
Project Location	Name of the location of the project	**Reference No. :** CM-PEC-D-0019-2015	

WBS ID	Activity Description	Unit	Quantity (A)	Unit Rate(Amount / Unit) (example; $ /cu.m)				Amount ($ or any unit currencies)
				Material	Labor	Others (contingency)	Total	
				(B)	(C)	(D)	(E) B+C+D	(A) x (E)
	Concreting of Floor Slab	cu.m.	10					

The tabulation above is based on the assumptions of the following;

- Unit Rate For Materials (example; $ / cubic meters)
  - Current price per unit given by vendors or updated Amount per unit from commercial data.
  - Derived from detailed estimate using direct counting of the materials, applying formulas considering a portion of area or as a whole.
  - Is the value of Amount ($, peso, euro)per unit (cubic meter, linear meter, square foot etc.)
  - Expressed in $ / linear meter, euro /square foot etc.
- Unit Rate For labour (example; $ / cubic meters, Salary per unit accomplished)
  - Current labor amount per unit given by vendors or updated Amount per unit from commercial data or industry pricing.
  - Derived from detailed estimate using labor rates, applying formulas, established parameters like man-hours (MH).

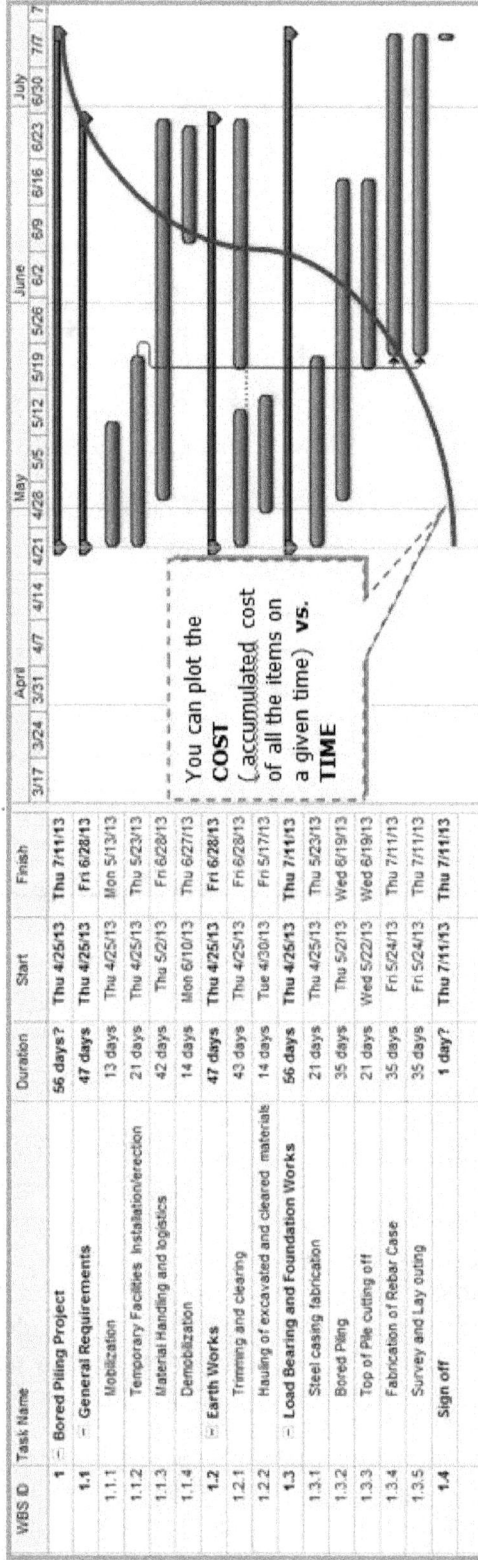

Cost Performance Baseline - (S-Curve)

Company Address :
Telephone :
Fax :
Email : info@
Website : www.

Template ID: PT-C-003
Date Prepared : 02/28/15
Revision : 000
Pages : 1 of 1
Reference No. : CM-PEC-D-0019-2015

Project	Name of the Project
Project Package	Name of the package / phase of the project
Project Location	Name of the location of the project

WBS ID	Task Name	Duration	Start	Finish
1	Bored Piling Project	56 days?	Thu 4/25/13	Thu 7/11/13
1.1	General Requirements	47 days	Thu 4/25/13	Fri 6/28/13
1.1.1	Mobilization	13 days	Thu 4/25/13	Mon 5/13/13
1.1.2	Temporary Facilities Installation/erection	21 days	Thu 4/25/13	Thu 5/23/13
1.1.3	Material Handling and logistics	42 days	Thu 5/2/13	Fri 6/28/13
1.1.4	Demobilization	14 days	Mon 6/10/13	Thu 6/27/13
1.2	Earth Works	47 days	Thu 4/25/13	Fri 6/28/13
1.2.1	Trimming and clearing	43 days	Thu 4/25/13	Fri 6/28/13
1.2.2	Hauling of excavated and cleared materials	14 days	Tue 4/30/13	Fri 5/17/13
1.3	Load Bearing and Foundation Works	56 days	Thu 4/25/13	Thu 7/11/13
1.3.1	Steel casing fabrication	21 days	Thu 4/25/13	Thu 5/23/13
1.3.2	Bored Piling	35 days	Wed 5/2/13	Wed 6/19/13
1.3.3	Top of Pile cutting off	21 days	Wed 5/22/13	Wed 6/19/13
1.3.4	Fabrication of Rebar Case	35 days	Fri 5/24/13	Thu 7/11/13
1.3.5	Survey and Lay outing	35 days	Fri 5/24/13	Thu 7/11/13
1.4	Sign off	1 day?	Thu 7/11/13	Thu 7/11/13

You can plot the **COST** (accumulated cost of all the items on a given time) **vs. TIME**

This illustration is for illustrative only and not intended to portray any construction projects, scope and description or not representing any specific ways to organize, plan of any type of construction projects.

Quality Management Plan		**Date Prepared:** 02/28/15	**Template ID:** PT-Q-001
Project	Name of the Project	**Revision :** 000	**Pages :** 1 of 1
Project Package	Name of the package / phase of the project		
Project Location	Name of the location of the project	**Reference No. :** CM-PEC-D-0021-2015	

Stakeholders:

Name	Organization	Role	Responsibilities	Duty Date
Pier John	Pier Engineering and Consultants			

Quality Assurance Plan*:*

Quality Control Plan*:*

Quality Improvement Plan*:*

Deliverables:

Category	Deliverables	Requirements	Reference	Comments (Date when to measure)

Quality Metrics*:*

Quality Reports and documents*:*

Company Address :
Telephone :
Fax :
Email : info@
Website : www.

Quality Metrics

Template ID:	PT-Q-002
Date Prepared :	02/28/15
Revision :	000
Pages :	1 of 3
Reference No. :	CM-PEC-D-0022-2015

Project	Name of the Project
Project Package	Name of the package / phase of the project
Project Location	Name of the location of the project

ID	Category	Item	Description	Method of Measurements	Metrics	Reference	Statistical Sampling
PP-01	Bored Pile	Concrete	Cast in place concrete pile (bored pile)	Compressive Test	3,000 psi (@28 days)	Structural Plan	• 5 Sets of cylinder at 3 piles / day
				Slump	100mm (max.)	Structural Plan / Structural Specification	• For each batch of concrete • 6 cu.m which ever is lesser
		Reinforcing Steel	Bored pile reinforcing steel	Tensile (Fy) 12mm dia. Bar and larger	413.7Mpa (60 ksi)		2.5 Tons per diameter per kind
				10mm dia. bar And smaller	276 Mpa (40 ksi)		2.5 Tons per diameter per kind
				Bending	No Crack		2.5 Tons per diameter per kind
PP-02e	Concrete Works , supply, fabrication, delivery and erection	Reinforcing Steel		Tensile (Fy) 12mm dia. Bar and larger	413.7Mpa (60 ksi)	Structural Plan / Structural Specification	2.5 Tons per diameter per kind
		Reinforcing Steel		10mm dia. bar And smaller	276 Mpa (40 ksi)		2.5 Tons per diameter per kind
				Bending	No Crack		2.5 Tons per diameter per kind

Company Address :
Telephone :
Fax :
Email : info@
Website : www.

Date Issue :	02/28/15	Pages :	2 of 3
Reference No. :		CM-PEC-D-0022-2015	
		Revision No. : 000	

Quality Metrics

ID	Category	Item	Description	Method of Measurements	Metrics	Reference	Statistical Sampling
PP-02e	Concrete Works , supply, fabrication, delivery and erection	Concrete	Curbs and slab on grade	Compressive Test	3,000 psi (@ 28 days)	Structural Plan / Structural Specification	• 3 Sets of 5 Samples per day of pouring or
				Slump	100 mm (max.)		150 cu.m concrete poured Or 500 sq.m slab or walls
				Temperature	35 degrees Celsius (max)		• For each batch of concrete (min) 10 cu. Yard (max)
			Pile Cap/ Tie Beam/ Footing	Compressive Test	3,000 psi (@ 28 days)		• For each batch of concrete (min) 10 cu. Yard (max)
				Slump	100 mm (max.)		Same as above
				Temperature	35 degrees Celsius (max)		Same as above
			Beam /Slab	Compressive Test	3,000 psi (@ 28 days)		Same as above
				Slump	100 mm (max.)		Same as above
				Temperature	35 degrees Celsius (max)		Same as above

Quality Metrics

	Date Issue :	Pages :
	02/28/15	3 of 3
	Reference No. :	
	CM-PEC-D-0022-2015	
	Revision No. : 000	

ID	Category	Item	Description	Method of Measurements	Metrics	Reference	Statistical Sampling
PP-02e	Concrete Works , supply, fabrication, delivery and erection	Concrete	Column Shear wall	Compressive Test	3,000 psi (@ 28 days)		Same as above
				Slump	100 mm (max.)		Same as above
				Temperature	35 degrees Celsius (max.)		Same as above
			Lean Concrete	Compressive Test	1,000 psi (@ 28 days)		Same as above
				Slump	100 mm (max.)		Same as above
				Temperature	35 degrees Celsius (max.)		Same as above

	Company Address :
	Telephone :
Your Logo here!	Fax :
	Email : info@
	Website : www.

Organizational Chart		Date Prepared : 02/28/15	Template ID: PT-HR-001
Project	Name of the Project	Revision : 000	Pages : 1 of 1
Project Package	Name of the package / phase of the project		
Project Location	Name of the location of the project	Reference No. : CM-PEC-D-0023-2015	

ORGANIZATIONAL CHART - Project Management Team

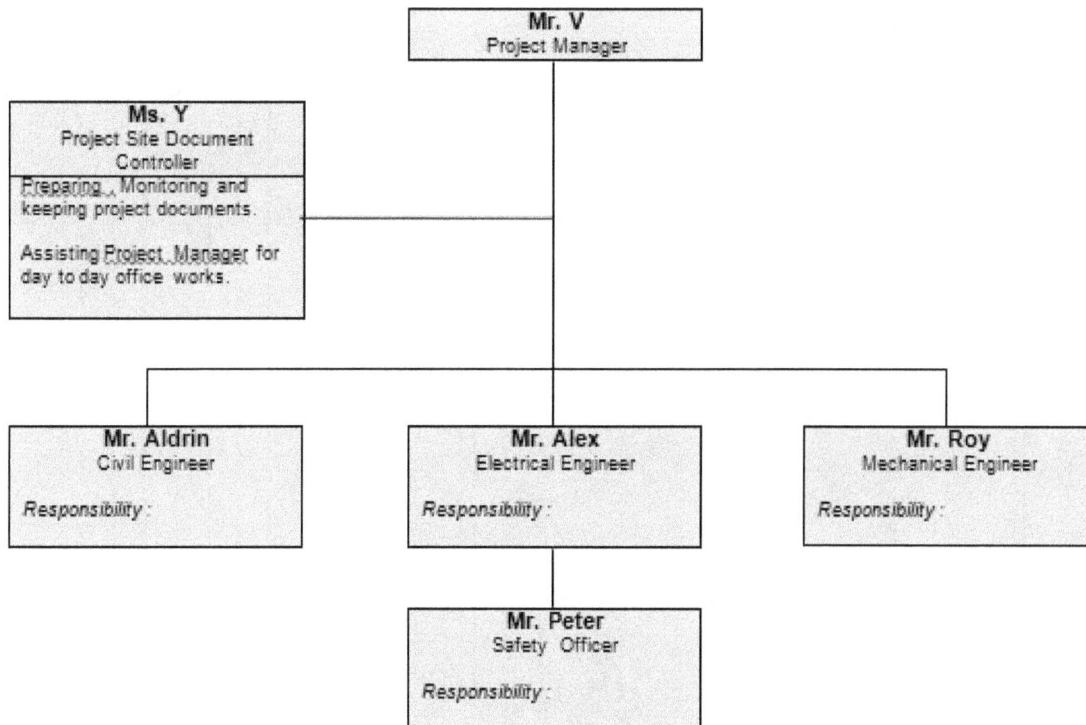

Your Logo here!

Responsibility Assign Matrix

		Date Prepared : 02/28/15	Template ID: PT-HR-002
Project	Name of the Project	**Revision :** 000	**Pages :** 1 of 1
Project Package	Name of the package / phase of the project		
Project Location	Name of the location of the project	**Reference No. :** CM-PEC-D-0024-2015	

R = Responsible, Person that performs the work

A = Accountable, Person that capable to answer that the requirements of the activity or work packages is acceptable

C = Consult, Person that has necessary data or information to execute and finish the required activity or work package

I = Inform, Person's to inform when the activity or work packages is complete

ID	Category	Activity	Description	Name 1	Name 2	Name 3	Name 4

Company Address :
Telephone :
Fax :
Email : info@
Website : www.

Human Resource Plan

		Date Prepared: 02/28/15	**Template ID:** PT-HR-003
Project	Name of the Project	**Revision :** 000	**Pages :** 1 of 4
Project Package	Name of the package / phase of the project		
Project Location	Name of the location of the project	**Reference No. :** CM-PEC-D-0025-2015	

Roles and Responsibility:

Roles	Responsibility	Authority	Competence / Ability	Duty Schedule	
				Start	End

Project Organizational Chart: *(see separate sheet attached – Organizational Chart)*

	Company Address :
	Telephone :
	Fax :
	Email : info@
	Website : www.

	Date Issue : 02/28/15	Pages : 2 of 4
Human Resource Plan	**Reference No.:** CM-PEC-D-0025-2015	
	Revision No. : 000	

Staffing Management Plan:

Staff Acquisition						
Category	**Role**	**Status**		**Location**	**Cost**	
		In house	outsource		weekly	Equivalent monthly

Human Resource Histogram

Your Logo here!

Company Address :
Telephone :
Fax :
Email : info@
Website : www.

Date Issue : 02/28/15	Pages : 3 of 4
Reference No.: CM-PEC-D-0025-2015	
Revision No. : 000	

Human Resource Plan

Staff Release	

Training		Awards	
Date		Date	

Human Resource Plan

Date Issue :	Pages :
02/28/15	4 of 4

Reference No.:
CM-PEC-D-0025-2015

Revision No. : 000

Compliance
(Regulations, Contract and Policy)

Human Resource Safety Provisions

Company Address:
Telephone:
Fax:
Email: info@
Website: www.

Template ID : PT-HR 004
Revision: 000

Reference No. : CM-PEC-D-0026-2015   Date: February 28, 2015

Page 1 of 1

To	:	**NAME OF HIRED EMPLOYEE**
Project	:	**DESIGNATED PROJECT**
Subject	:	**EMPLOYMENT CONTRACT - TEMPORARY AS PROJECT TO PROJECT BASIS ONLY**

This serves as your temporary employment contract, bounded by the following terms and condition.

I.   DESIGNATION   : Specify role and of the hired employee and which project will he be working on.

II. DURATION   : Specify duration of the project, including the provision for termination.

III. COMPENSATION   : Specify amount of salary per week or per month that he will be getting, including provision of benefits and allowances.

IV. RESPONSIBILITIES : Specify list of employee's responsibilities as required to the project.

Signed and agreed upon this 1st day of September, 2013, at New Hampshire Building, New York.

Company Name

By: Conforme:

NAME OF COMPANY REPRESENTATIVE   **NAME OF EMPLOYEE**
President   Employee

This Temporary Employment Contract is for illustrative purposes only and not intended to portray any actual contracts for employment. To deal with this, please consult your Legal Department or Human Resource Department.

Company Address:
Tel :0000000
Fax : 0000000
Email : info@
Website: www

Template ID: PT-HR-005
Revision: 000

Reference No. : CM-PEC-D-0027-2015

Date: February 28, 2015

To	:	**PROJECT MANAGER**
Project	:	**NAME OF THE PROJECT**
Subject	:	**CONTRACT EXPIRATION NOTICE**

The contracts of staff members listed below are due to expire.

Staff Member's Name	Role	Project Assignment	Date of Effectivity

Please advise us on or before thirty (30) days prior to their contracts status.

Prepared by:

Signature:

_____

Administrative Officer

Template ID: PT-HR-006
Revision : 000
Reference No. : CM-PEC-D-0028-2015
Date : February 28, 2015
Page 1 of 1

To	:	**PROJECT MANAGER**
Project	:	**NAME OF THE PROJECT**
Subject	:	**CONTRACT EXTENSION REQUEST**

I recommend here with for your approval, the extension of the contract of the following staff members listed below.

Staff Member's Name	Role	Contract Expiration	Proposed Extension		Reason of Extension
			Start	**End**	

Prepared by: Approved by:

_____

Project Manager

Cc: Administrative Officer
Project File

Company Address:
Tel :0000000
Fax : 0000000
Email : info@
Website: www

Template ID: PT-HR-007
Revision : 000

Reference No. : CM-PEC-D-0029-2015

Date: February 28, 2015

Page 1 of 1

Attention	:	**STAFF MEMBER'S NAME**
		Role
Project	:	**Name of the project**
Project Package	:	PP 01 – General Civil and Architectural Works
Location	:	Project Location
Subject	:	**NON RENEWAL OF CONTRACT**

Dear **STAFF MEMBER'S NAME,**

We would like to inform you that we are not going to renew your contract for the project mentioned above. Your contract will be terminated on *Date and Time.*

Respectfully Yours,

_____

Signature

_____

Printed Name / Date

_____

Administrative Officer

Noted by:

_____

Signature

_____

Printed Name / Date

_____

Project Manager

Company Address:
Tel :0000000
Fax : 0000000
Email : info@
Website: www

Template ID: PT-HR-008
Revision: 000

Reference No. : CM-PEC-D-0030-2015

Date: February 28, 2015

Attention	:	**STAFF MEMBER'SNAME**
		Role
Project	:	**Name of the project**
Project Package	:	PP 01 – General Civil and Architectural Works
Location	:	Project Location
Subject	:	**CONTRACTEXTENSION**

Dear **STAFF MEMBER'S NAME,**

Please be advised that we are extending your contract for the project mentioned above. Your contract will be effective ***Date and Time.*** Previous Contract conditions remain unchanged and your current role will be the same.

Kindly affix your signature with the space provided below for your conformity.

Respectfully Yours,

_____
Printed Name / Date

_____
Project Manager

Conform;

_____
Printed Name / Date

_____
Staff Member's Role

Communication Management Plan		**Date Prepared :** 02/28/15	**Template ID:** PT-COM-001
Project	Name of the Project	**Revision :** 000	**Pages :** 1 of 3
Project Package	Name of the package / phase of the project		
Project Location	Name of the location of the project	**Reference No. :** CM-PEC-D-0031-2015	

Information / Message :(Details of information or message to be communicated)

Information Description	Method	Stakeholder					Frequency
		Receiver			Sender		
		Name	Organization	Reason for distribution	Name	Organization	

Your Logo here!

Communication Management Plan

Date Issue : 02/28/15	Pages : 2 of 3
Reference No.: CM-PEC-D-0031-2015	
Revision No. : 000	

Resources:

Category	Description	Schedule	Budget	Reference / Provision

Flow charts and Work flows:

	Company Address :
	Telephone :
	Fax :
	Email : info@
	Website : www.
Communication Management Plan	**Date Issue:** 02/28/15	**Pages:** 3 of 3
	Reference No.: CM-PEC-D-0031-2015	
	Revision No.: 000	

Glossary:

Terminology	Definition

Risk Management Plan		**Date Prepared :** 02/28/15	**Template ID:** PT-R-001
Project	Name of the Project	**Revision :** 000	**Pages :** 1 of 4
Project Package	Name of the package / phase of the project		
Project Location	Name of the location of the project	**Reference No. :** CM-PEC-D-0032-2015	

Risks Analysis:

Qualitative Risk Analysis

Risks:(use this also as a tool and technique to identify risk, explore more possible risks)

ID	Category			Description
	Internal			
		Funds		
		Costs		
		Time / Schedule		
		Resources		
			Material	
			Equipment	
			Manpower	
		Contractor		
		Sponsor		
	External			
		Suppliers		
		Sub - Contractor		
		Government		
		Regulatory		
		Market		
		Cultural		
		Customer		
		Nature		

Risk Management Plan

ID	Category			Description
			Weather	
			Acts of Nature	
	Technical			
		Compatibility / Interface		
		Requirements (Technology, Performance)		
		Quality		
		Scope		
	Project Management			
		Knowledge		
		Experience		
		Planning		
			Estimates	
			Communication	
			Human Resource	

Stakeholder:

Roles	Organization	Responsibility

	Company Address :
	Telephone :
	Fax :
	Email : info@
	Website : www.

Risk Management Plan

Date Issue : 02/28/15	Pages : 3 of 4
Reference No.: CM-PEC-D-0032-2015	
Revision No. : 000	

Definition: (Risk probability and Impact)

Schedule: (When and How often the risk management process will be performed)

Budget: (Resources used, funds to be utilize for risk management, like mitigating risk budget and Contingency reserve.)

Tracking: (How the risks will be audited and recorded)

Company Address :
Telephone :
Fax :
Email : info@
Website : www.

Your Logo here!

Risk Register

Project	Name of the Project
Project Package	Name of the package / phase of the project
Project Location	Name of the location of the project

Date Prepared :	02/28/15
Template ID:	PT-R-002
Revision :	000
Pages :	1 of 3
Reference No. :	CM-PEC-D-0033-2015

ID	Category	Probability Score	Impact Score	Priority Score	Description	Response Owner	Response Date	Status
	Internal							
	Funds							
	Costs							
	Time / Schedule							
	Resources							
	• Material							
	• Equipment							
	• Manpower							
	Contractor							
	Sponsor							

Company Address :
Telephone :
Fax :
Email : info@
Website : www.

Pages : 2 of 3

Date Issue : 02/28/15
Reference No. : CM-PEC-D-0033-2015
Revision No. : 000

Your Logo Here!

Risk Register

ID	Category	Probability Score	Impact Score	Priority Score	Response				Status
					Description	Owner	Date		
	External								
	Suppliers								
	Sub - Contractor								
	Government								
	Regulatory								
	Market								
	Cultural								
	Customer								
	Nature								
	• Weather								
	• Acts of Nature								

ID	Category	Probability Score	Impact Score	Priority Score	Response				Status
					Description	Owner	Date		
	Technical								
	Compatibility/Interface								
	Requirements (technology , performance)								
	Quality								
	Scope								

Risk Register

Company Address :
Telephone :
Fax :
Email : info@
Website : www.

Date Issue : 02/28/15	Pages : 3 of 3
Reference No. : CM-PEC-D-0033-2015	
Revision No. : 000	

ID	Category	Probability Score	Impact Score	Priority Score	Description	Response		Status
						Owner	Date	
	Project Management							
	Knowledge							
	Experience							
	Planning							
	• Estimates							
	• Communication							
	• Human Resource							

Company Address :
Telephone :
Fax :
Email : info@
Website : www.

Owner Supplied Materials

		Date Prepared : 02/28/15	Template ID: PT-P-001
Project	Name of the Project	**Revision :** 000	**Pages :** 1 of 1
Project Package	Name of the package / phase of the project		
Project Location	Name of the location of the project	**Reference No. :** CM-PEC-D-0034-2015	

No.	Description	Brand/Specification	Quantity	Unit	Date Needed on Site	Remarks

Procurement Management Plan

		Date Prepared: 02/28/15	Template ID: PT-P-002
Project	Name of the Project	**Revision :** 000	**Pages :** 1 of 2
Project Package	Name of the package / phase of the project		
Project Location	Name of the location of the project	**Reference No. :** CM-PEC-D-0034-2015	

STAKEHOLDER: (person involved in procurement, manage, documents and executing procurement contracts)

Role	Responsibility (Describe the responsibility in the procurement process)	Authority level (define the authority level for, costs, technical, decisions, changes, transactions)
Project Manager		
Team		
Procurement Manager		

TYPE OF CONTRACT : (State the contract type to be used)

DOCUMENTATION : (List all the necessary procurement documents and integration process to organization procurement documents, provision for OSME)

ESTIMATES : (independent estimates to be use, evaluation or selection.)

SCHEDULE : (Establish how the seller will integrate their supply or services schedule with the project schedule)

PERFORMANCE : (Establish how the seller will integrate their performance reports and all necessary submittals to procurement process)

WBS : (Establish how the seller will adopt and maintain and develop the project WBS with their integration of supplies or services

	Company Address :
	Telephone :
	Fax :
	Email : info@
	Website : www.

Your Logo here!

	Date Issue :	Pages :
Procurement Management Plan	02/28/15	2 of 2
	Reference No.:	
	CM-PEC-D-0034-2015	
	Revision No. : 000	

BONDS OR INSURANCES: (describe the bonds / insurance to be carried out on the contract as part of mitigating the risk).

ASSUMPTION : (Establish necessary assumption to be used for procurement process.)

CONSTRAINTS : (Establish necessary constraints to be used for procurement process.)

RISKS : (Establish Risks associated with procurement process)

Company Address :
Telephone :
Fax :
Email : info@
Website : www

Procurement Statement of Work

		Date Prepared: 02/28/15	Template ID: PT-P-003
Project	Name of the Project	**Revision :** 000	**Pages :** 1 of 1
Project Package	Name of the package / phase of the project		
Project Location	Name of the location of the project	**Reference No. :** CM-PEC-D-0036-2015	

ID	Category	Item Description	Unit	Quantity

Documents :(Attached detailed documents in a separate sheets, if contained large paper size pages)

Document Number	Description	Number of pages	Reference Number
1	Quantities		
2	Work Schedule		
3	Technical Specification		
4	Reference Drawing		

	Company Address :
	Telephone :
	Fax :
	Email : info@
	Website : www.

Request For Information (RFI)		RFI No. 000	Date Prepared : 02/28/15	Template ID: PT-P-004
Project	Name of the Project	**Revision :** 000		**Pages :** 1 of 1
Project Package	PP 01 – General Civil and Architectural Works			
Project Location	Name of the location of the project	**Reference No. :** CM-PEC-D-0037-2015		

SELLER'S / ARCHITECT'S / ENGINEERS COMPANY NAME
Company Address

ATTENTION : **SELLER'S / ARCHITECT'S / ENGINEER'SNAME**
Role

SUBJECT : *Sample Only :* ***Roof Framing Specification***

Description :
*Sample Only :*May we request the complete description of the chord WT 4x15.5 (in x lb/ft)for the main roof truss. Can we useW8 x 31 (in x lb/ft) and cut into half to get the said section?

Instruction / Comment :

_____
Name and Signature Date

Prepared by:

_____
Signature

_____
Printed Name / Date

_____
Role / Organization or Company

Company Address:
Tel:0000000
Fax: 0000000
Website: www

Template ID: PT-P-005
Revision: 000

Reference No. : CM-PEC-D-0038-2015

Date: February 28, 2015

Seller's / Bidder's Company Name
Address

Attention	:	**Seller's Name or Company representative**
		Role
Project	:	**Name of the project**
Project Package	:	PP 01 – General Civil and Architectural Works
Location	:	Project Location
Subject	:	INVITATION FOR PREQUALIFICATION OF SELLER

Gentlemen,

We are pleased to invite you to participate in the prequalification of seller/bidder for the **supply of materials, labor, tools, equipment and supervision to complete Project Package 01 (PP 01)** General Civil and Architectural Works for the above mentioned project, below are the documents to be submitted.

Technical;

- Records of previous projects (similar and not similar projects).
- Company background, details and location.
  - Business Permit
  - Contractor's License
  - Company Certifications (ISO etc)
- Personnel to be assign, details and experiences.

Financial;

- Total Current Assets and Liabilities
- Bank Certificates
(Above financial data is to be certified by Accountant or Auditor)

Company Address:
Tel:0000000
Fax: 0000000
Website: www

Sealed Technical and Financial documents in two(2) copies each and marked **Application for Prequalification for _Project Name_** must be submitted and stamped received at the office of;

Attention: **MR. ABC (**Owner's Representative / Document Receiver)
Company Address

Not later than, 2:00pmon Date _____.

The Project Manager reserves the right to reject any of the application for prequalification or any part thereof, to waive any informality there in and to select qualified seller or bidder that would be found in its opinion to be most reliable to the project manager.

Please signify your interest for pre-qualification for bid by signing on the space below and send back to _Pier Engineering and Consultants_ thru email at _info@pierengineeringandconsultants.com,_ or fax,_00000000_, not later than 10:00 am, Date _____.

Respectfully Your,

PIER JOHN
Project Manger

Invitation to pre-qualify for bid,
received and confirmed intent by;

_____
Signature

_____
Printed Name / Date

_____
Role / Organization or Company

Company Address:
Tel:0000000
Fax: 0000000
Website: www

Template ID : PT-P-006
Revision : 000

Reference No. : CM-PEC-D-0039-2015

Date: February 28, 2015

Page 1 of 2

Seller's / Bidder's Company Name
Address

Attention	:	**Seller's Name or Company representative** Role
Project	:	**Name of the project**
Project Package	:	PP 01 – General Civil and Architectural Works
Location	:	Project Location
Subject	:	**INVITATION FOR BID (IFB)**

Gentlemen,

This is to inform you that you have been prequalified and invite you to participate in the bidding for the **supply of materials, labor, tools, equipment and supervision to complete Project Package 01 (PP 01)** General Civil and Architectural Works for the proposed" *name of the project*" located in" project location".

Structural, Architectural plans and all related project documents shall be available for pick up on *"specify time and date"* at the office of;

> **MR. ABC (**Owner's Representative / Designer etc.)
> Company Address
> Contact Numbers

Upon payment of non-refundable cash deposit of **USD (Amount in words), $ (Amount in figures).**

Sealed Technical and Financial documents in two(2) copies each and marked " **Proposal For PP-01GeneralCivil and Architectural Works-***Project Name*" must be submitted and stamped received at the office of;

> Attention: **MR. ABC(**Owner's Representative / Document Receiver)
> Company Address
>
> Not later than, 2:00pmon Date _____.

The Owner / Sponsor reserves the right to reject any of the Bids or any part thereof, to waive any informality there to award the contract to any of the Bidders / Sellers select that would be found in its opinion , to be most reliable and advantageous to the owner .

A pre bid conference will be scheduled on , "**Date , Day**" at the office of **Company Name of Consultant or Sponsor** at "**Time**" .Please prepare your written clarifications prior to this meeting date.

Please signify your interest to bid by signing on the space below and send back to **Company Name of Consultant or Sponsor** thru email at *email address* or fax No.___ not later than 10:00 am , Date _____.

Respectfully Yours,

PIER JOHN
Project Manger

Invitation for bid received and confirmed intent to bid by ;

_____
Signature

_____
 Printed Name / Date

_____
Role / Organization or Company

Your Logo here!

Company Address :
Telephone :
Fax :
Email : info@
Website : www.

Pre – Qualification Criteria

Date Prepared : 02/28/15	Template ID: PT-P-007
Revision : 000	Pages : 1 of 5
Reference No.: CM-PEC-D-0040-2015	

Project	Name of the Project
Project Package	Name of the package / phase of the project
Project Location	Name of the location of the project

BIDDER/SELLER/CONTRACTORS
COMPANY X (Name of the Sellers Company)

DESCRIPTION	POINTS	Projects	Project Cost	Equivalent points
I. EXPERIENCE AND CAPABILITY OF FIRM	30			
a.) Previous Project Records (Similar projects)	20			20
1.) With similar projects in the last 5 years (**20 pts.**)				
2.) Without similar projects but with comparable nature (**15 pts.**)				
b.) Repeat engagement with the same client/customer as Seller/Contractor	5			5
c.) Geographical consideration for intended project	5			5
Location of office or satellite office is within the region (**5 pts.**)				
Location of office or satellite office is outside the region (**2 pts.**)				
Sub - Total I	30			30

Company Address :
Telephone :
Fax :
Email : info@
Website : www.

Pre – Qualification Criteria

Date Issue : 02/28/15
Reference No. : CM-PEC-D-0040-2015
Revision No. : 000
Pages : 2 of 5

Your Logo here!

II. QUALITY OF PERSONNEL TO BE ASSIGNED	30	NUMBER OF YEARS	30
1. Project Manager / Project Engineer			
1.1 Experience of the Project Manager	20	(example entry)	(example)
15 years and above (20 pts.)		Project Manager - 14 years (put 10 points)	10
10 - 14 years (10 pts.)			
5 - 9 years (5 pts.)			
1.2 Experience of Project Engineer	5	(example entry)	(example)
10 years and above (5 pts.)		Project Engineer - 5 years(put 3 points)	3
5 - 9 years (3 pts.)			
1.2.1 Years in Company	5		
6 years and above (3 pts.)			
5 years and below (2 pts.)			
5 years and below (1 pt.)			

Company Address :
Telephone :
Fax :
Email : info@
Website : www.

Date Issue :	Pages :
02/28/15	3 of 5
Reference No. :	
CM-PEC-D-0040-2015	
Revision No. : 000	

Your Logo here!

Pre – Qualification Criteria

Project Engineer			
6 years and above (2 pts.)			
5 years and below (1 pt.)			
Sub - Total II		30	30

III. CONTRACTING CAPABILITIES		40	Year (latest)	40
1.1 Total Current Assets				
1.2 Total Current Liabilities				
1.3 Net Worth = TCA - TCL				
1.4 Approximate Cost of Project				
1.5 Maximum Contracting Capacity = Net Worth x 10				
1.6 Gross Contracting Capability = MCC x 0.30				
1.7 Equity = Net Worth x 10				
1.8 Net Financial Contracting Capability (NFCC)				

Company Address :
Telephone :
Fax :
Email : info@
Website : www.

Date Issue : 02/28/15	Pages : 4 of 5
Reference No. : CM-PEC-D-0040-2015	
Revision No. : 000	

Your Logo here!

Pre – Qualification Criteria

Conditions:

If the Net Financial Contracting Capability (NFCC) is equal to or greater than Estimated Cost of the project, the seller or the bidder is financially qualified.

If the NFCC is less than half of the Estimated Cost of the Project, the seller or the bidder is financially not capable or disqualified.

If the NFCC equals at least half of the Estimated Cost of the Project, the seller's or the bidder's is financially un capability or insufficient. To satisfy the requirements , direct loans , financier or other instruments from banking/financial institutions is needed in an amount equal or at least one and a half (1.5) times the deficiency in net worth. Otherwise, the bidder is financially disqualified.

If the NFCC equals at least half of the Estimated Cost of the Project, the seller's or the bidder's is financially un capability or insufficient. To satisfy the requirements , direct loans , financier or other instruments from banking/financial institutions is needed in an amount equal or at least one and a half (1.5) times the deficiency in net worth. Otherwise, the bidder is financially disqualified.

Sub - Total III				40	40

Pre – Qualification Criteria

Date Issue : 02/28/15	Pages : 5 of 5
Reference No. : CM-PEC-D-0040-2015	
Revision No. : 000	

TOTAL POINTS I+II+III	100			100

To qualify For Bid the Seller/Contractor should have a total points of not less than 75points.

Prepared by:

Signature :

Name :

Role and Organization :

Step 3

Executing

STEP 3 : EXECUTING

The Executing Process Group is the third process group with the purpose of applying processes to complete the work defined in our project management plan , executing is the coordination of all resources like , people , materials and equipment and the necessary activities in accordance with the specified project management plan.

Flow Chart - Project Management process is not always sequential or performed in identical sequence.

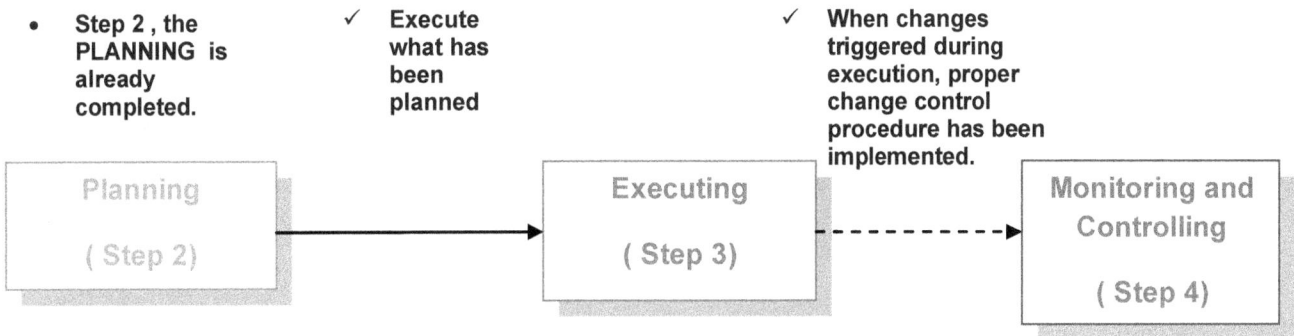

- **Step 2 , the PLANNING is already completed.**

✓ **Execute what has been planned**

✓ **When changes triggered during execution, proper change control procedure has been implemented.**

Planning	Executing	Monitoring and Controlling
(Step 2)	(Step 3)	(Step 4)

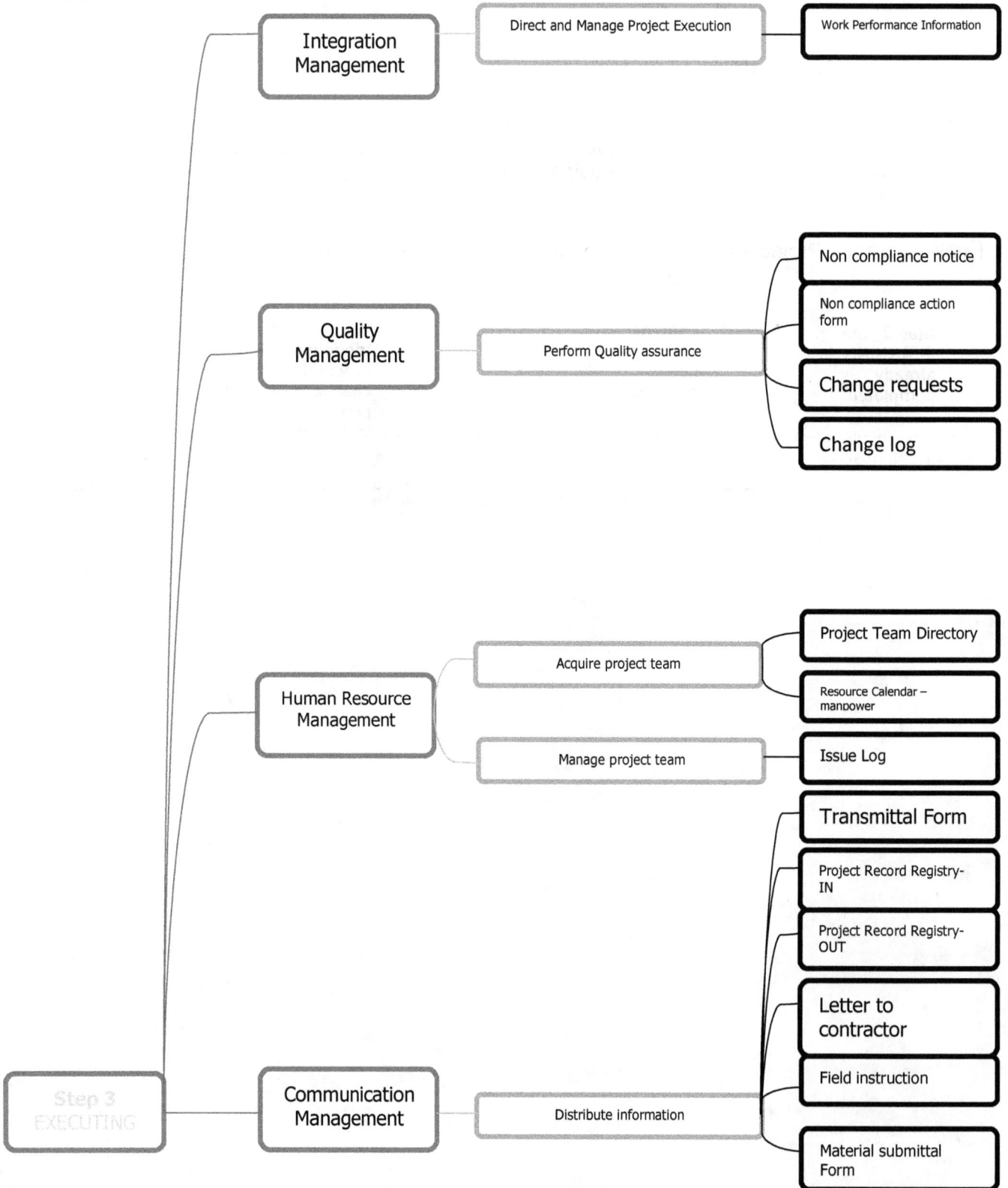

Mapping:

Integration Management	Direct and Manage Project Execution	Work Performance Information

Quality Management	Perform Quality assurance	Non compliance notice
		Non compliance action form
		Change requests
		Change log

Human Resource Management	Acquire project team	Project Team Directory
		Resource Calendar – manpower
	Manage project team	Issue Log

		Transmittal Form
		Project Record Registry-IN
		Project Record Registry-OUT
Step 3 EXECUTING → **Communication Management**	Distribute information	**Letter to contractor**
		Field instruction
		Material submittal Form

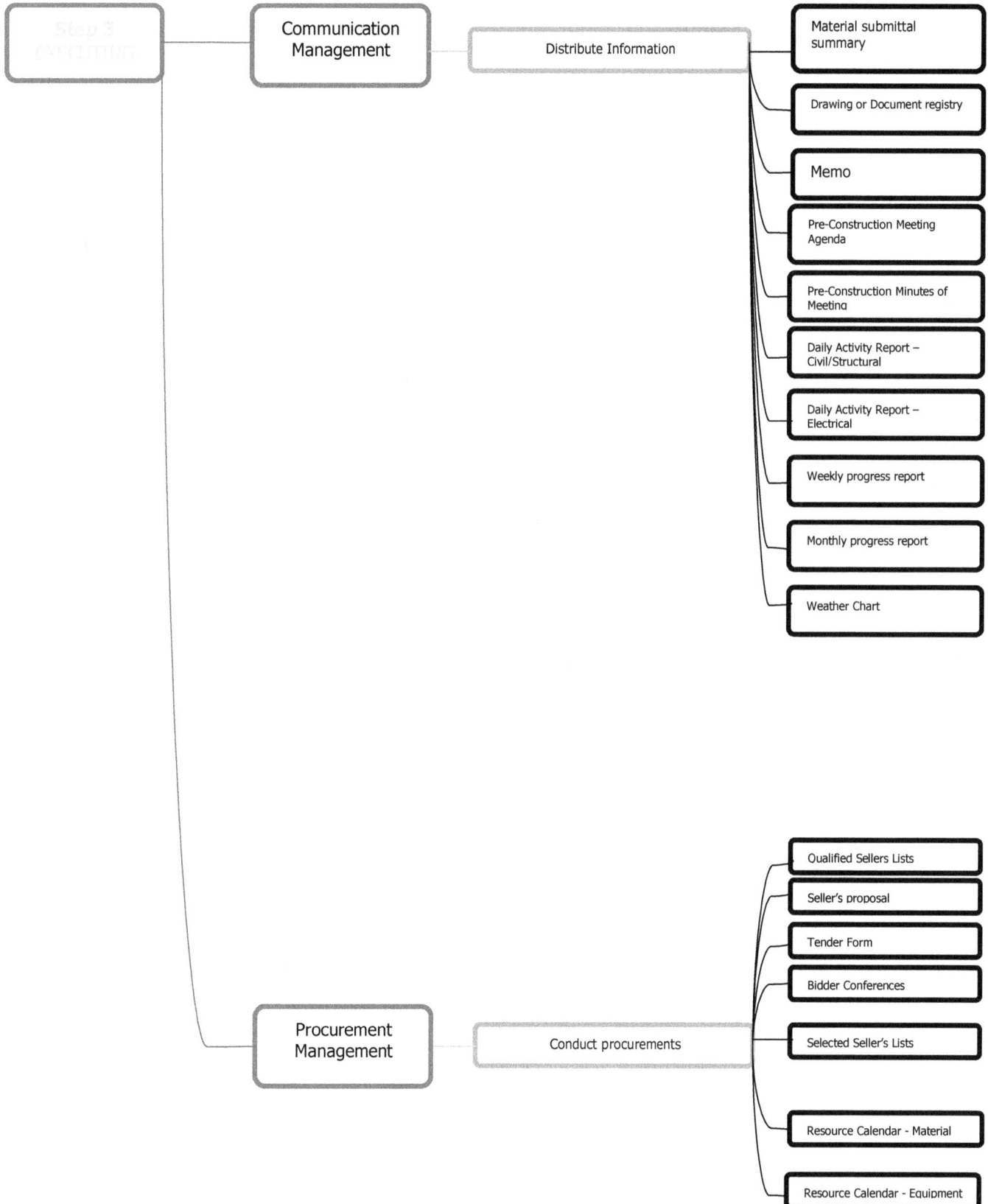

```
┌─────────────┐     ┌─────────────────┐     ┌──────────────────────┐     ┌──────────────────────────┐
│   Step 3    │     │  Communication  │     │ Distribute Information│     │ Material submittal        │
│  EXECUTING  │─────│   Management    │─────│                       │     │ summary                   │
└─────────────┘     └─────────────────┘     └──────────────────────┘     └──────────────────────────┘
                                                                          ┌──────────────────────────┐
                                                                          │ Drawing or Document registry│
                                                                          └──────────────────────────┘
                                                                          ┌──────────────────────────┐
                                                                          │ Memo                      │
                                                                          └──────────────────────────┘
                                                                          ┌──────────────────────────┐
                                                                          │ Pre-Construction Meeting  │
                                                                          │ Agenda                    │
                                                                          └──────────────────────────┘
                                                                          ┌──────────────────────────┐
                                                                          │ Pre-Construction Minutes of│
                                                                          │ Meeting                   │
                                                                          └──────────────────────────┘
                                                                          ┌──────────────────────────┐
                                                                          │ Daily Activity Report –   │
                                                                          │ Civil/Structural          │
                                                                          └──────────────────────────┘
                                                                          ┌──────────────────────────┐
                                                                          │ Daily Activity Report –   │
                                                                          │ Electrical                │
                                                                          └──────────────────────────┘
                                                                          ┌──────────────────────────┐
                                                                          │ Weekly progress report    │
                                                                          └──────────────────────────┘
                                                                          ┌──────────────────────────┐
                                                                          │ Monthly progress report   │
                                                                          └──────────────────────────┘
                                                                          ┌──────────────────────────┐
                                                                          │ Weather Chart             │
                                                                          └──────────────────────────┘

                                                                          ┌──────────────────────────┐
                                                                          │ Qualified Sellers Lists   │
                                                                          └──────────────────────────┘
                                                                          ┌──────────────────────────┐
                                                                          │ Seller's proposal         │
                                                                          └──────────────────────────┘
                                                                          ┌──────────────────────────┐
                                                                          │ Tender Form               │
                                                                          └──────────────────────────┘
                                                                          ┌──────────────────────────┐
                                                                          │ Bidder Conferences        │
                                                                          └──────────────────────────┘
                    ┌─────────────────┐     ┌──────────────────────┐     ┌──────────────────────────┐
                    │  Procurement    │     │ Conduct procurements  │     │ Selected Seller's Lists   │
                    │   Management    │─────│                       │     └──────────────────────────┘
                    └─────────────────┘     └──────────────────────┘     ┌──────────────────────────┐
                                                                          │ Resource Calendar - Material│
                                                                          └──────────────────────────┘
                                                                          ┌──────────────────────────┐
                                                                          │ Resource Calendar - Equipment│
                                                                          └──────────────────────────┘
```

WORK PERFORMANCE INFORMATION (WPI)

Is a dynamic document which is routinely collected as the project progresses. It involves data and information about the actuals results of performance or progress of the project.

WPI has many uses in the project management, such as scope, time, cost, quality, communication, risk, and procurement management. It is often created during the third step of managing projects.

Templates : WPI , Non-Compliance Notice(NCN), Non-Compliance Action(NCA)

CHANGE REQUEST

Change request is a document used to formally ask for any minor or major changes in the project, including scope, schedule, costs, staffing requirements, policies, and procedures of the performing organization for the project. It also includes preventive or corrective actions and defect repair. This document is being created during the third step of managing projects.

Template : Change Request

CHANGE LOG

Change log is a list or summary of all submitted change requests used to monitor and track the status of project changes. This registry is a dynamic document and to be updated throughout the project.

Template : Change Log

PROJECT TEAM DIRECTORY

Is part of the project staff assignment. This document is a list of members of the project, including the complete information of the member like email, mobile numbers, and organization. This document is being created during the third step of managing projects.

Hot Tip
- Post site team directory inside the office (contractor, designer, consultants, and owner's representatives) for easy communication.

Template : Project Team Directory,

RESOURCE CALENDAR

Resource Calendar is a document that specifies the availability, schedule, and equivalent quantity of resources. This document is being created during the third step of managing projects.

Template : Resource Calendar-Manpower

ISSUE LOG

Is a list of issues of human resource that may occur throughout the project. Issues are circumstances that are under discussion or unsettled. These are the results of different points of view and disagreements. The issue log is usually created during the third step of managing projects.

INFORMATION DISTRIBUTION

Information distribution is the process of providing necessary information available to stakeholders, and is often performed throughout the project duration. During the distribution of required information to stakeholders, it is best to track the important information, such as emails and hard copies with transmittal form to be signed by the receiver of the document. The information distribution is being done during the third step of managing projects.

Templates : Transmittal Form, Project Records Registry-IN, Project Records Registry-OUT, Letter To Seller, Field Instructions (FI), Material Submittal Form, Material Submittal Summary, Drawing or Document Registry, Memo , Pre-construction meeting agenda *(use for construction project)*, Pre-construction minutes of meeting*(use for construction project)*

DAILY ACTIVITY REPORT

Daily Activity Report is being used in the construction industry for progress reporting on the daily basis and it is bring up into summary level for project status report , daily activity report is being prepared by team member and to be submitted to project manager as detailed , summary or broad form depending on the needs of the project , this document is very useful for risk , safety , environmental issues and project progress , also , along with this report is the weather chart and being filled up on the daily basis .The daily activity report and project weather chart is being created in the third step or the STEP 3 in managing projects

when time extension is the issue , some will fall under force majeure and one of the references for hours affected will be the weather chart , so keep a record of the weather chart on hourly basis.

Templates : Daily Activity Report Civil and Structural, Daily Activity Report Electrical, Weekly Progress Report, Monthly Progress Report

QUALIFIED SELLERS LIST

Is a type of list derived from conducting procurements process. The sellers that are included in the list are already prequalified or prescreened from previous project performance, company, or organization capability. This document is often done during the third step of managing projects.

Template : Qualified Sellers List

SELLERS PROPOSAL

A seller proposal is a document submitted by the sellers in response to the procurement documents given to them. This will be the basic information that the evaluation body will be used in selecting qualified sellers. This document is usually done during the third step of managing projects.

Template : Sellers Proposal , Tender Form,

BIDDER CONFERENCES

Bidder conferences, pre-bid conferences, and contractor conferences are formal meetings that are conducted prior to submission of proposals or bids. The meeting is often attended by the buyer or owner, project management team, and the prospective sellers. This meeting is usually held during the third step of managing projects.

Template : Selected Seller's List

PROCUREMENT CONTRACT

Is a mutually binding legal document or agreement where the seller provides specified requirements, products, or services, and in which the buyer has to compensate the seller. This is in the form of simple or complex document, or just a simple purchase order (P.O.) form. The procurement contract is to be awarded to selected seller.

This document is usually done during the third step of managing projects.

Template: Resource Calendar Materials, Resource Calendar Equipment.

Company Address :
Telephone :
Fax :
Email : info@
Website : www.

Work Performance Information

		Date Prepared : 02/27/15	Template ID: ET-I-001
Project	Name of the Project	Revision : 000	Pages : 1 of 1
Project Package	Name of the package / phase of the project		
Project Location	Name of the location of the project	Reference No. : CM-PEC-D-0041-2015	

ID	Category	Deliverables	Activity	Schedule		Cost	Supplier / Contractor	Reference	Status
				Started	Finished	Amount			

Company Address :
Telephone :
Fax :
Email : info@
Website : www.

Concrete Pouring

		Date Prepared : 09/01/13	Template ID: ET-Q-001
Project	Name of the Project	Revision : 000	Pages : 1 of 1
Project Package	Name of the package / phase of the project	Reference No. :	
Project Location	Name of the location of the project	CM-PEC-D-0042-2013	

Time	Truck No.	Slump		Temperature		Concrete Class	Structure Location and Description	Concrete Cylinder ID	Comments
		Required	Reading	Required	Reading				

Contractor's Quality Control :

Signature : _____ /Date
Name :
Organization :

Verified / Checked :

Name / Signature: _____ /Date
Inspector/ Consultant

Noted: _____ /Date
Project Manager

Your Logo here!

Company Address :
Telephone :
Fax :
Email : info@
Website : www.

Concrete Cylinder Test Log

		Date Prepared : 09/01/13	Template ID: ET-Q-002
Project	Name of the Project	Revision : 000	Pages : 1 of 1
Project Package	Name of the package / phase of the project		
Project Location	Name of the location of the project	Reference No.: CM-PEC-D-0043-2013	

Cylinder ID	Location / Member	Date of Pouring	Date of Testing	Age (Days)	Strength(psi) @ 28 days		Test Results		Remarks
					Strength	Reference	Strength	Reference	

Contractor's Quality Control :

Signature :
Name : _____ /Date
Organization :

Verified / Checked :

Name / Signature: _____ /Date
Inspector/ Consultant

Noted: _____ /Date
Project Manager

STEEL REINFORCEMENT TEST LOG

Project :

Project Package :

Date :

Item No.	Sample Description	Location / Member	Date Submitted	Date of Testing	Test in TENSION			Test in BENDING		Remarks
					Test Results - Fy (Mpa)		Required Strength - Fy (Mpa)	Test Results Bending Angle 180 degrees	Standard Specs.	
					sample 1	sample 2 average				
1	28mm Grade 60 - W		06/02/12	06/02/12	447	447	414	No Crack	Non - Crack	satisfactory

prepared by: **Name**
Contractor's Quality Control

checked / verified: **Name**
Inspector /Consultant

Noted by: **Name**
Project Manager

Company Address :
Telephone :
Fax :
Email : info@
Website : www.

Batch Plant Inspection

		Date Prepared : 09/01/13	Template ID: ET-Q-004
Project	Name of the Project	**Revision :** 000	**Pages :** 1 of 1
Project Package	Name of the package / phase of the project		
Project Location	Name of the location of the project	**Reference No. :** CM-PEC-D-0045-2013	

No.	Category	Rating	Comments
1	Coarse Aggregate Stockpile		
2	Fine Aggregate Stockpile		
3	Cement Warehouse / Trucks		
4	Cement Silo		
5	Transit Mixers		
6	Admixture warehouse / facilities		
7	Source of Water		
8	Water storage tanks		
9	Material Receiving area		
10	Offices / Service Area		
11	Housekeeping		
12	Plant Capability and Performance		

Attached Plant Photographs:

Rating :

Excellent	:	4
Good Condition	:	3
Fair	:	2
Poor	:	1

Inspected by:

_____

Name / Signature

Role

Organization

Your Logo here!

Non Compliance Notice (NCN)

Date Prepared : 02/28/15	**Template ID:** ET-Q-005	

Project	Name of the Project	**Revision :** 000	**Pages :** 1 of 1
Project Package	Name of the package / phase of the project		
Project Location	Name of the location of the project	**Reference No. :** CM-PEC-D-0046-2015	

Contractor's/Seller's Company Name Company A	**Contractor's/Seller's Name : In charge** Engineer X **Role :** Project Manager
WBS ID :	**Scope / Work Package / Requirement:** Retaining Wall	**Reference :** (Drawing , Specification , Contract provision etc.)

No.	Description	Structure location /Particular	Current Status / Condition
1	Spacing of vertical Reinforcement	Retaining Wall at Grid line 1 and Grid line D-G	Installation of reinforcement steel bar

Issued by ;

_____
QC / Inspector

Noted by ;

_____
Project Manager

Received by ;

_____
Contractor / Seller

Date Received ;

_____

Pier Engineering & Consultants

Project Managers • Engineers • Construction

Company Address:
Tel :0000000
Fax : 0000000
Email : info@
Website: www.

Non Compliance Action Form	**Date Prepared :** 02/28/15	**Template ID:** ET-Q-006
Project — Name of the Project	**Revision :** 000	**Pages :** 1 of 1
Project Package — Name of the package / phase of the project		
Project Location — Name of the location of the project	**Reference No. :** CM-PEC-D-0047-2015	

Contractor's/Seller's Company Name Company A	**Contractor's/Seller's Name : In charge** Engineer X **Role :** Project Manager
WBS ID :	**Scope / Work Package / Requirement:** Retaining Wall	**Reference :** (Drawing, Specification, Contract provision etc.)

Corrective Action / Defect Repair

No.	Description	Action	Date of Completion	Inspector / Consultant's Comment
1	Spacing of vertical Reinforcement	Re work and corrected into specified spacing		

Certified by ;

_____ / Date _____
Contractor's Quality Control

Verified by ;

_____ / Date _____
Contractor's Project Manager

Received / Approved ;

_____ / Date _____
Inspector / Consultant

Noted by ;

_____ / Date _____
Project Manager

Company Address :
Telephone :
Fax :
Email : info@
Website : www.

Change Request Form

		Date Prepared : 02/28/15	Template ID: ET-Q-007
Project	Name of the Project	**Revision :** 000	**Pages :** 1 of 2
Project Package	Name of the package / phase of the project		
Project Location	Name of the location of the project	**Reference No. :** CM-PEC-D-0048-2015	

Change Number 01	**Change Category**				
	[ ] Scope	[ ] Quality	[ ] Schedule	[ ] Cost	[ ] Documents

Requesting Person			
Name	Role	Organization	Signature

Proposed Change	
Description	Justification

Impact	
Scope	Enumerate and describe the impact of change on the project scope
Quality	Enumerate and describe the impact of change on the project quality
Schedule	Enumerate and describe the impact of change on the project schedule
Cost	Enumerate and describe the impact of change on the project cost

Attachments / Supporting Documents

Evaluator or Reviewed by:		
_____ Name & Signature _____ Role & Organization	[ ] Submit detailed estimates On _____ [ ] Submit Drawings [ ] Attach other documents. **Other Comments ;**	[ ] Approved and proceed to Change Order Authorization [ ] Rejected **References ;** Contracts Drawings Specification , etc.

Your Logo here!

Change Request Form

Date Issue : 02/28/15	Pages : 2 of 2
Reference No.: CM-PEC-D-0048-2015	
Revision No. : 000	

Change Control Board				
Name	Role	Organization	Signature	Date

Company Address :
Telephone :
Fax :
Email : info@
Website : www..

Change Log	Date Prepared : 02/28/15	Template ID: ET-Q-008
Project	Name of the Project	**Revision :** 000	**Pages :** 1 of 1
Project Package	Name of the package / phase of the project		
Project Location	Name of the location of the project	**Reference No. :** CM-PEC-D-0049-2015	

Change Request No.	Change Description	Submitted		Status			Comments
		Date	Responsible	Approve	Reject	Date	

Project Team Directory

		Date Prepared : 02/28/15	Template ID: ET-HR-001

Project	Name of the Project	Revision :	Pages :
Project Package	Name of the package / phase of the project	000	1 of 1
Project Location	Name of the location of the project	Reference No. : CM-PEC-D-0050-2015	

Name	Role	Address	Contact Numbers			Email
			Telephone	Mobile	Fax	

Resource Calendar - Manpower

		Date Prepared : 02/28/15	Template ID: ET-HR-002
		Revision : 000	Pages : 1 of 1
		Reference No. : CM-PEC-D-0051-2015	

Project	Name of the Project
Project Package	Name of the package / phase of the project (**Bored Piling Works**)
Project Location	Name of the location of the project

weeks

Item No.	Role	1	2	3	4	5	6	7	8	9	10	11	12
1	Project Manager												
2	Project Engineer / Resident Engineer												
3	Material Engineer												
4	Safety Officer												
5	Health Personnel												
6	Foreman												
7	Mason												
8	Carpenter												
9	Labourer												
10	Rigger												
11	Driver												
12	Operator												

This illustration is for illustrative only and not intended to portray any construction projects , scope , description of any type of construction projects .

Company Address :
Telephone :
Fax :
Email : info@
Website : www.

Transmittal Form

		Date Prepared: 02/28/15	Template ID: ET-COM-001
Project	Name of the Project	**Revision :** 000	**Pages :** 1 of 1
Project Package	Name of the package / phase of the project		
Project Location	Name of the location of the project	**Reference No. :** CM-PEC-D-0052-2015	

TO :
ATTENTION :
CC :

FROM :
ROLE :
ORGANIZATION :   **CONTACT #** :

[ ] FOR YOUR INFORMATION   [ ] FOR YOURETENTION   [ ] FOR YOUR QUOTATION

[ ] FOR YOUR ACTION   [ ] FOR YOUR COMMENTS/CHECKING & RETURN   [ ] EXTRA COPIES AS REQUESTED

[ ] FOR YOUR APPROVAL   [ ] FOR YOUR SIGNATURE & RETURN   [ ] AS REQUESTED

[ ] FOR COORDINATION   [ ] CHARGEABLE

Sent Via			
[ ] Courier / Mail	[ ] Email /Internet	[ ] Hand	[ ] Self Collect

Number of Prints			Serial No.	Revision	Description
Paper	Tracing Paper	Size			

Remarks :

Acknowledgement			
I / We received the above in good order except serial number **0** as marked "x"			
Company Stamp	Name of Receiver	Signature	Date

Project Records Registry – IN

Your Logo here!

Project Records Registry – IN		Date Prepared: 02/28/15	Template ID: ET-COM-002
Project	Name of the Project	**Revision :** 000	**Pages :** 1 of 1
Project Package	Name of the package / phase of the project		
Project Location	Name of the location of the project	**Reference No. :** CM-PEC-D-0053-2015	

No.	Reference No.	Category	Description	Date Received	Comments

Company Address :
Telephone :
Fax :
Email : info@
Website : www.

Project Records Registry - OUT

| | | Date Prepared: 02/28/15 | Template ID: ET-COM-003 |

Project	Name of the Project	Revision : 000	Pages : 1 of 1
Project Package	Name of the package / phase of the project		
Project Location	Name of the location of the project	Reference No. : CM-PEC-D-0054-2015	

No.	Reference No.	Category	Description	Date Forwarded	Comments

Template ID: ET-COM-004
Revision: 000

Reference No.: CM-PEC-L-0001-2015

Date: February 28, 2015

Page 1 of 1

CONTRACTOR'S COMPANY NAME
Address

Attention   **:CONTRACTOR'S NAME/COMPANY REPRESENTATIVE**
Role

Project   **:NAME OF THE PROJECT**

Project Package   : **GENERAL CONSTRUCTION WORKS**

Location   :Project Location

Subject   **:SUB- PUMPS / PROTECTION COVER AND SITEINCHARGE DURING HOLY DAYS**

Hi _____ ,

As part of preventive action for possible rain (unpredictable) damage during Holydays , please provide the following as needed on site ;

1. Protective Cover (blue sheet) for sloped area as shown in the picture.
2. Sub-pump
3. Staff / Personnel to check the site condition.

All of the above mention requirements were discussed on site together with Engr._____.

For Your compliance,

Very truly yours,

Name
Consultant's company name

Your LOGO Here!

Company Address:
Tel :0000000
Fax : 0000000
Email : info@
Website: www

Template ID: ET-COM-005
Revision: 000
Reference No. : CM-PEC-L-0002-2015
Date: February 28, 2015
Page 1 of 1

Project : Name of the project	Field Instruction Number :
Project Package : PP 01 – General Civil and Architectural Works	Date : Feb 15, 2015
Location :	
SUBJECT :	
Instructions :	
Remarks :	

Prepared by :   **Noted by:**

_____   _____

Signature   Project Manager

_____
Printed Name / Date

_____
Role (Field Inspector)/ Organization

Company Address :
Telephone :
Fax :
Email : info@
Website : www.

Material Submittal		Date Prepared: 02/28/15	Template ID: ET-COM-006
Project	Name of the Project	**Revision :** 000	**Pages :** 1 of 1
Project Package	Name of the package / phase of the project		
Project Location	Name of the location of the project	**Reference No. :** CM-PEC-D-0055-2015	

Category :Civil / Structural   **Work Package** :Blind Drain

Item No.	Material Description	Brand Model (Technical Data)	Action		Remarks
			Code	Date	
1	GeoTextile	B-20 GeoTextile			

Having reviewed this submittal , we certify that it conforms to requirements and condition of the contract

_____
Contractor / Seller

Action Code :
A - Approved   ,   **B** - Approved with comments
C - Revise and Re-submit , **D** - Disapproved

Project Manager's Comment ;

_____
Signature

_____
Name and Organization

Engineer's /Architect's Comment ;

_____
Signature

_____
Name and Organization

Sponsor's / Customer's Comment ;

_____
Signature

_____
Name and Organization

Reference No.: CM-PEC-D-0056-2015

MATERIAL SUBMITTAL SUMMARY

Project :

Project Package :

Date :

No.	Control No.	Revision	Submittal Subject	PLANNED (Contractor's Submission)	ACTUAL (Contractor's Submission)	Consultant's Comment	Approval Status
1	S-M / 0064	0	B-20 Geotextile - Brand Name/ Distributors Name		05/22/15	06/06/15	B
2	S-M / 0001	0	Soil Poisoning Chemicals - Brand Name/ Distributors Name		05/18/15	06/06/15	B
3	S-M 0077/0082	1	Panel Boards & BusDuct - Brand Name/ Distributors Name		06/26/15	06/26/15	B
4							
5							
6							
7							
8							
9							
10							
11							

ACTION CODE / STATUS ; A- Approved ; B- Approved with Comments , C- Revise and Re-submit (Work may NOT PROCEED) , D- Disapproved

prepared by:

DRAWING REGISTRY

Project :

Project Package :

Date :

Item No.	WBS ID	Description	Sheet Number	Revision Number	Revision Date	Date received from designer	Date issued to Contractor	Size and Type	Purpose	Remarks
						Consultant (Project Management)				
1		BORED PILES	BP-0010					A1 (blueprint)	for bidding	
		Bored pile lay out	BP-0011					A1 (blueprint)	for bidding	
		Pile cap details	BP-0012					A3 (pdf)	for bidding	

prepared by:

Your LOGO Here!

Company Address:
Tel :0000000
Fax : 0000000
Email : info@
Website: www

Template ID: ET-COM-009
Revision: 000

Reference No.: CM-PEC-L-0003-2015

Date: February 28, 2015
Page 1 of 1

MEMO

TO	:	**ALLCONTRACTORS, SUB CONTRACTORS**
FROM	:	**NAME**
		PROJECT MANAGER
		ORGANIZATION
SUBJECT	:	**YOUR SUBJECT HERE**

Body of text here.

Respectfully Yours,

Signature:

_____

Project Manager Name

_____

Organization or Company Name

Company Address:
Tel :0000000
Fax : 0000000
Email : info@
Website: www

Template ID: ET-COM-010
Revision: 000

Reference No.: CM-PEC-D-0058-2015   Date: February 28, 2015

Project	:	**NAME OF THE PROJECT**	
Location	:	**PROJECT LOCATION**	
Subject	:	**PRE CONSTRUCTION MEETING AGENDA**	
Venue	:	**LOCATION OF THE MEETING**	Time :

1.0 Project Organization
    1.1   Introduction of the project team
            1.1.1   Owner
            1.1.2   Contractor
                   1.1.2.1 CV of Personnel
                   1.1.2.2 Site In Charge (in the absence of Contractor's CM)
                   1.1.2.3 Organizational Chart
            1.1.3   Designers/Consultants
            1.1.4   Project Management Consultants

2.0 Requirement for Building Permit (by owner or Contractor)
    2.1   Permit Plans *(Sets , sealed)*
    2.2   Permit Forms
    2.3   Environmental Compliance Certificate

3.0 Project Implementation Schedule
    3.1   Bar Chart with S-Curve
    3.2   PERT – CPM
            3.2.1 For Contractor's Planner/Scheduler

4.0 Construction Drawings and Specifications
    4.1   Issuance of final construction drawings and specifications
            4.1.1   Owner
            4.1.2   Contractor
            4.1.3   Project Manager

5.0 Construction Management System
    5.1   Communication System
            5.1.1   Communication Flow
            5.1.2   Email and File Sharing System
    5.2   Construction Standard Templates

YOUR LOGO HERE!

Company Address:
Tel :0000000
Fax : 0000000
Email : info@
Website: www

Template ID: ET-COM-010
Revision: 000
Date: February 28, 2015
Page 2 of 3

Reference No. : CM-PEC-D-0058-2015

5.3   Approval turn around period for technical submittal

5.4   Quality Control Program
          5.4.1   Design Mix
          5.4.1.1 Batching Plant (with options/alternatives)
          5.4.2   Testing Laboratories *(QC Personnel)*

5.5   Environment , Health and Safety
          5.5.1   Regular Toolbox Meetings
          5.5.2   Hazard / Risk Identification and Mitigation
          5.5.3   Safety Officer - Full time
          5.5.4   Project Nurse - Full time

6.0 Construction Policies, Requirements

6.1   Site Access
          6.1.1   Gate and Pathway
          6.1.2   Coordination with Campus Security
              6.1.2.1 Security Agency
          6.1.3   Worker's ID/PPE/Uniform

6.2   Site Offices / Warehouse / Temporary Facilities
          6.2.1   Site Lay out
          6.2.2   PM site office requirement
          6.2.3   Site Status as of date

6.3   Construction Site Security

6.4   Material and or debris storage and disposal

6.5   Protection of existing structures / facilities

6.6   Campus Rules and Regulations
          6.6.1   Deliveries and Daily Access *(coordinate with owner's representative)*
          6.6.2   Working Time *(coordinate with the owner)*
          6.6.3   Other restrictions
          6.6.3.1 No Smoking
          6.6.3.2 Others
6.7   Construction Methodology
6.8   Schedule of Regular Construction Coordination Meetings

YOUR LOGO HERE!

Company Address:
Tel :0000000
Fax : 0000000
Email : info@
Website: www

Template ID :ET-COM-010
Revision : 000

Reference No. : CM-PEC-D-0058-2015

Date: February 28, 2015
Page 3 of 3

7.0 Other Matters

    7.1   Ground Rules

            7.1.1 Meetings

                    7.1.1.1 Switch off the Cell phone .

            7.1.2 Others

    7.2   Delivery of Materials (contractors responsibility)

    7.3   Temporary Utilities

    7.4   Full Time Basis - Site Personnel

            7.4.1   Civil and Structural Engineer

            7.4.2   Building Services Engineer

            7.4.3   Liaison Officer

            7.4.4   Safety Officer

            7.4.5   Planner

            7.4.6   QA/QC

            7.4.7   Survey Team

            7.4.8   QS

Prepared by:

_____

Name and Signature

Noted by:

_____

Project Manager

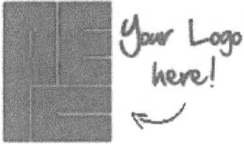

Company Address:
Tel :0000000
Fax : 0000000
Email : info@
Website: www

Template ID: ET-COM-011
Revision: 000

Reference No. : CM-PEC-D-0059-2015

Project	:	**NAME OF THE PROJECT**
Location	:	**PROJECT LOCATION**
Subject	:	**PRE CONSTRUCTION MINUTES OF MEETING**
Venue	:	**LOCATION OF THE MEETING**

ATTENDEES:

Name	-	Company Name	Name	-	Company Name
Name	-	Company Name	Name	-	Company Name
Name	-	Company Name	Name	-	Company Name

ACCOMPLISHMENT:

WBS ID	Work Package No.	Target Accomplishment	Actual Accomplishment	Slippage/ Advance	Equivalent Days
	Bored Piling				
	Architectural				

The meeting was called to order at TIME and the following items were discussed:

ITEM NO.	MATTERS DISCUSSED	RESPON-SIBLE	DUE DATE	REMARKS
1.0	**Project Organization**			
1.1	**Introduction of the project team**			
1.1.1	**Owner**			
1.1.2	**Contractor**			
1.1.3	**Designers/Consultants**			
1.1.4	**Project Management Consultant** and others will be mobilize upon construction on-progress			
2.0	**Requirement for Permits (by Owner)**			
2.1	**Building Permit**			

YOUR LOGO HERE!

Company Address:
Tel :0000000
Fax : 0000000
Email : info@
Website: www

Template ID :ET-COM-011
Revision : 000
Reference No. : CM-PEC-D-0059-2015
Date : February 28, 2015
Page 2 of 3

2.2	ECC			
3.0	**Project Implementation Schedule**			
3.1	**Bar Chart & S-curve**			
3.2	**PERT CPM**			
4.0	**Construction Drawings & Specifications**			
4.1	**For Construction Drawings &**			
5.0	**Construction Management System**			
5.1	**Communication System**			
5.2	**Construction Standard Templates**			
5.3	**Approval turn around period for technical submittal.**			
5.4	**Quality control program**			
5.5	**Environment, health & Safety**			

YOUR LOGO HERE!

Company Address:
Tel :0000000
Fax : 0000000
Email : info@
Website: www

Template ID :ET-COM-011
Revision : 000

Reference No. : CM-PEC-D-0059-2015

Date : February 28, 2015
Page 3 of 3

There being no other matters to be discussed the meeting was adjourned at TIME.

The Minutes of Meeting is the recollection of what transpired at the meeting. If no corrections/amendments or other information within two (2) days from the receipt of the minutes, this will be considered reflective of the accounts of what transpired and therefore considered approved.

Prepared by:

_____

Name and Signature

.

Noted by:

_____

Project Manager

Company Address :
Telephone :
Fax :
Email : info@
Website : www.

Daily Activity Report

			Date Prepared: 02/28/15	Template ID: ET-COM-012
Day : Monday	**Weather :** Rainy	**Temperature :** 20 C		
Project	Name of the Project		**Revision:** 000	**Pages :** 1 of 1
Project Package	Name of the package / phase of the project			
Project Location	Name of the location of the project		**Reference No. :** CM-PEC-REP-0001-2015	
Category	*Write the category of the trade – Civil or Structural*			

ACTIVITIES

ID	Category	Description	Accomplished	Variance	Comments

RESOURCES

ID	Manpower / People	Comments

ID	Materials	Comments

ID	Equipment	Comments

BASELINE

Quality		Cost / Funds		
Variance	Actions	Planned to spent	Actual spent	Variance and Comments

ISSUES   :
RISKS   :

Prepared by   :   (Name) _____
                      __ (Organization) _____
                      __ (Role) _____

www.PierEngineeringandConsultants.com

Daily Activity Report

			Date Prepared: 02/28/15	Template ID: ET-COM-013
Day : Monday	**Weather :** Rainy	**Temperature :** 20 C		
Project	Name of the Project		**Revision :** 000	**Pages :** 1 of 1
Project Package	Name of the package / phase of the project			
Project Location	Name of the location of the project		**Reference No. :** CM-PEC-R-0002-2015	
Category	Electrical Works			

ACTIVITIES

ID	Category	Description	Accomplished	Variance	Comments

RESOURCES

ID	Manpower / People	Comments

ID	Materials	Comments

ID	Equipment	Comments

BASELINE

Quality		Cost / Funds		
Variance	Actions	Planned to spent	Actual spent	Variance and Comments

ISSUES   :

RISKS   :

Prepared by   :   (Name)_____
                   __ (Organization)_____
                   __ (Role)_____

Project Name

Perspective View

PROJECT WEEKLY UPDATE
Date:

PIER ENGINEERING and CONSULTANTS
Your Logo here!

Project Managers • Consulting Engineers

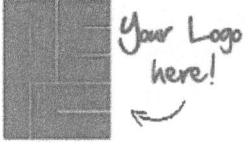

Company Address:
Tel :0000000
Fax : 0000000
Email : info@
Website: www

Template ID : ET-COM-017
Revision : 000

Your Logo
here!

A. Accomplishment Update

WBS ID	Work Package / Description	Planned %	Actual %	Variance	Status as of date (current activity)	Comments
	Bored Pile	9.94	0.13	-9.81	Fabrication of Rebar Boring of pile holes	**Schedule:** 19 Calendar days- delayed **Cost :**
	Structural Steel					**Schedule:** **Cost :**
	Architectural					**Schedule:** **Cost :**
	Electrical					**Schedule:** **Cost :**
	Other Items					**Schedule:** **Cost :**

B.   Project Update

Item No.	Description	Comments
1	Safety Issues	
2	Design	
3	Procurement	
4	Requirements	

C.   Progress Photos

Site Picture

Description

Site Picture

Description

Site Picture

Description

Project Name

Project Location

Perspective View

PROGRESS REPORT NO. 01

Covering Period of *Month – Month*, 2013

PIER ENGINEERING and CONSULTANTS

Project Managers • Consulting Engineers

Your Logo here!

www.PierEngineeringandConsultants.com

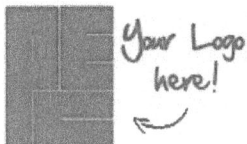

Company Address:
Tel :0000000
Fax : 0000000
Email : info@
Website: www

Template ID: ET-COM-018
Revision: 000

Reference No. : CM-PEC-R-0007-2015

OWNER'S COMPANY NAME
Address

Attention	:	**OWNER'S NAME or COMPANY REPRESENTATIVE** *Role*
Project	:	**NAME OF THE PROJECT** *Project Location*
Subject	:	**MONTHLY STATUS REPORT NO.1**

Sir/Ma'am,

We are submitting herewith the **Monthly Status Report No. 01** for the proposed **Name of the project** covering the period from **Date, Year to Date Year.**

We hope you will find everything in order.

Thank you.

Very truly yours,

NAME
CONSULTANT'S COMPANY NAME-Resident Engineer

Noted by:

NAME
CONSULTANT'S COMPANY NAME-Project Manager

Here are the contents of the Monthly Report but not limited to the following;

     I.   **GENERAL SUMMARY**

    II.   **CONSTRUCTION**

        A. Accomplishment Update
        B. Work in progress and Milestone

    III.   **DESIGN UPDATE**

    IV. PROCUREMENT

        A. Contractors and Suppliers List
        B. Owner Supplied Materials and Equipment Lists (OSME Lists)

    V. FINANCIAL STATUS

    VI. REQUIREMENTS UPDATE

        A. Permits and Licenses

    VII. ATTACHMENTS

        A. Progress Photos
        B. Schedule
        C. Weather Charts
        D. Minutes of Meeting

Qualified Sellers Lists

		Date Prepared : 02/19/15	Template ID: ET-P-001
Project	Name of the Project	**Revision :** 000	**Pages :** 1 of 1
Project Package	Name of the package / phase of the project		
Project Location	Name of the location of the project	**Reference No. :** CM-PEC-D-0060-2015	

Work Package (WP)	Description	Seller/Bidder's Company Name	Seller/Bidder's Contact Details	Contact Person	Remarks
WP-01	General Civil/ Architectural Works	Seller No.1 **Company Name:**	Company Details (Address, Telephone, website) :	Name : Role: Mobile No. Email:	
		Seller No.2 **Company Name:**	Company Details (Address, Telephone, website) :	Name : Role: Mobile No. Email:	
		Seller No.3 **Company Name:**	Company Details (Address, Telephone, website) :	Name : Role: Mobile No. Email:	
WP-02	Bored Piling Works	Seller No.1 **Company Name:**	Company Details (Address, Telephone, website) :	Name : Role: Mobile No. Email:	
		Seller No.2 **Company Name:**	Company Details (Address, Telephone, website) :	Name : Role: Mobile No. Email:	

Company Address :
Telephone :
Fax :
Email : info@
Website : www.

Seller Proposal
(Water Proofing Proposal)

		Date Prepared: 02/28/15	Template ID: ET-P-002
Project Package	*Water Proofing*	Revision : 000	Pages : 1 of 2
Project	Name of the project		
Project Location	Name of the location of the project	Reference No. : CM-PEC-D-0061-2015	

OWNER REPRESENTATIVE
Address

Attention   :   **OWNER'S NAME or REPRESENTATIVE**
Role

Dear Sir/Ma'am,

In compliance with your request for proposal on the above project package, we are pleased to submit the following for your consideration:

Item No.	Location	Area (sq.m)	Specification	Unit Price / sq.m.	Amount ($)
1	**Concrete Slab**	10,000	(Cementitous/Capillary) *B15* Slurry		
Total					$

Amount in Words:

Terms of Payment : 30% Down Payment , balance thru weekly progress billing payable within seven (7) days upon receipt of each billing.

Guarantee   :   *B15* Slurry - Waterproofing system against leak for a period of Five (5 years).

Scope of work   : **OSMOSEAL (Osmosis/ Crystallization)**

1. Mobilization
2. Scrape/ Remove existing loose mortar, dirt and other foreign matters.

3. Construction joints and perimeter of drain pipes with polyurethane sealant .cracks should be out to 1/4" x 1/4" prior to filling with polyurethane sealant. Allow to dry.

4. Saturate routed area and leave damp for application.

5. Apply two (2) coating of *B15* Slurry Cementitous Crystallization Waterproofing on the entire prepared area.

Should you have any queries, please do not hesitate to call us and we will be glad to discuss this with you at your most convenient time.

Very truly yours,

_____
SELLER'S NAME AND SIGNATURE
Role
SELLER'S COMPANY NAME

CONFORME:

Signature :
By   : Owner's Name or Representative
Date   :

	Tender Form	**Date Prepared:** 02/28/15	**Template ID:** ET-P-003
Project	Name of the Project	**Revision :** 000	**Pages :** 1 of 2
Project Package	Fire Protection, Plumbing, HVAC, Electrical, Testing and Commissioning		
Project Location	Name of the location of the project	**Reference No. :** CM-PEC-D-0062-2015	

Company Address :
Telephone :
Fax :
Email : info@
Website : www.

Your Logo here!

1   I/We, having read and examined the tender documents and drawings, do hereby offer to execute and complete, in accordance with the Conditions of Contract and other Contract Documents, the whole of the *Project Package* as follows -

For completion of the whole of The Works within your set time as stated in your Conditions of Contract (Appendix A) for the sum of $

....

(\$) including all Taxes.

2.   I/We agree that should any discrepancy occur between the amounts written in words and in figures entered upon the Form of Tender, the amount written in words will be used.

3   I/We agree to abide by this tender for the period of 90 days from the date fixed for receiving the same and shall remain binding upon me/us and maybe accepted at any time before the expiration of that period.

4   If my/ our tender is accepted, I/we will provide you with a performance bond, callable upon demand, either in cash or by way of an approved insurance bond or banker's guarantee of an amount equal to 20% of the Contract Sum within 7 days of the date of acceptance of my/our tender.

5   I/We agree that should any arithmetical or obvious pricing errors be discovered before acceptance of this offer in the priced tender documents submitted by me/us, then these errors shall be corrected in order that the corrected total of the Final Summary equates with the amount entered upon the Form of Tender in accordance with the following procedure:

The net total of such errors, whether addition or net omission, will be calculated as a percentage of the corrected total of the Final Summary and all unit rates and prices throughout the Bills of Quantities shall be considered as reduced or increased, as the case may be, by such percentage.

6.   I/We undertake, in the event of your acceptance, to execute with you a formal contract embodying all the conditions and terms contained in this offer and until such execution, the conditions and terms contained in this offer shall bind me/us and your acceptance shall constitute a binding contract between you and me/us.

7.   I/We understand that you are not bound to accept the lowest or any tender.

8   Unless directed to the contrary, I/we undertake to commence The Works immediately but not later than 7 days from issuance of Letter of Award.

9.   I/We acknowledge receipt of Tender Addendum/Bulletin No(s) _____ to the Tender Documents and confirm that the contents of the said Tender Addenda/Bulletin form an integral part of the tender submitted by me/us.

10.   If there shall be a wage increase during the project period the total labor adjustment per one USD (1.00) increase in minimum wage or compulsory allowances to be paid by the Owner to the Contractor is a lump sum of USD: _____, which shall be applied to the remaining works after the wage increase and according to the provisions of the Contract Documents.

11.   I/We confirm that all bonds, insurances, permits and other fees are to be shouldered by our company unless stated in the Contract Documents to be by Owner. All penalties incurred shall be my/our responsibility.

12.   I/We will complete the whole Works within _____ (___) calendar months inclusive of all Sundays and holidays.

Signature   :
in the capacity of   :   *Name of the Owner or Representatives*
Duly authorized to sign tenders on behalf of   :   *Company Name*
Company Address   :
Date Signed   :

Witness   :   *Name of Witness*
Address   :
Date Signed   :

Please seek advice from your attorney or legal advisor when dealing with this tender form.

Your Logo here!

SELLECTED SELLER'S LIST

Project :
Project Package :
Project Location :

Date prepared :

Project Package No.	Description	Bidders / Contractor/Supplier	Cost			Total Amount	Remarks
			Materials	Labor	Equipment		
PP-01	Civil / Architectural Works	Company X					
PP-02	Plumbing and Sanitary	Company X					
PP-03	Mecahnical	Company X					
PP-04	Electrical	Company X					
PP-05	Fire Protection System	Company X					
PP-06	CCTV Surveillance System	Company Y					
PP-07	Structured Cabling	Company Z					
PP-08	Audio / Video and Equipment	Company A					
PP-09	Fire Alarm and Detection System	Company B					

Prepared by:

Your Logo Here!

Resource Calendar – Materials

		Date Prepared :	Template ID:
		02/28/15	ET-P-007
Project	Name of the Project	Revision :	Pages :
Project Package	Name of the package / phase of the project	000	1 of 1
Project Location	Name of the location of the project	Reference No.:	
		CM-PEC-D-0064-2015	

| No. | Description of Material | Make | | Required at Site | Planned Submittal Date | 1st Submittal Date | RESPONSE | Approval Date | | Order Date | | Actual Delivery Date at Site | Remarks/Status |
		Specified	Proposed					Reqd	Actual	Planned	Actual		
1													
2													
3													
4													
5													
6													
7													
8													

STATUS : A- Approved, B- Approved with Comments, C- Revise and Re-submit , D- Disapproved

Prepared by:

Step 4

Monitoring and Controlling

Resource Calendar - Equipment

		Date Prepared : 02/28/15	Template ID: ET-P-008
Project	Name of the Project	Revision : 000	Pages : 1 of 1
Project Package	Name of the package / phase of the project (*Bored Piling Works*)		
Project Location	Name of the location of the project	Reference No. : CM-PEC-D-0065-2015	

Item No.	Equipment Description	No. of Units	_weeks_ 1	2	3	4	5	6	7	8	9	10	11	12
1	Boring Machine	2												
2	Generator Set	2												
3	Diesel Hammer	4												
4	Crawler Crane – 40 Tonner	2												
5	Feeder Crane – 25 Tonner	2												
6	Welding Machine	2												
7	Concrete Batching Plant	1												
8	Transit Mixer	3												
9	Concrete Vibrator	3												
10	Pay Loader	1												
11	Dump Truck	2												
12	Boom Truck	1												

This illustration is for illustrative only and not intended to portray any construction projects , scope , description of any type of construction projects .

www.ConstructionProjectManagementPro.com

STEP 4 : MONITORING AND CONTROLLING

Monitoring and Controlling is the fourth step in managing projects with the purpose of reviewing , monitoring and tracking of project progress and performance and compare it to a given baseline of the project management plan , monitoring the project gives an overview about the project performance and it will identify some areas of the project that needs additional attention , controlling contains preventive or corrective actions and assures that defined actions resolved the project issue .

Flow Chart - Project Management process is not always sequential or performed in identical sequence.

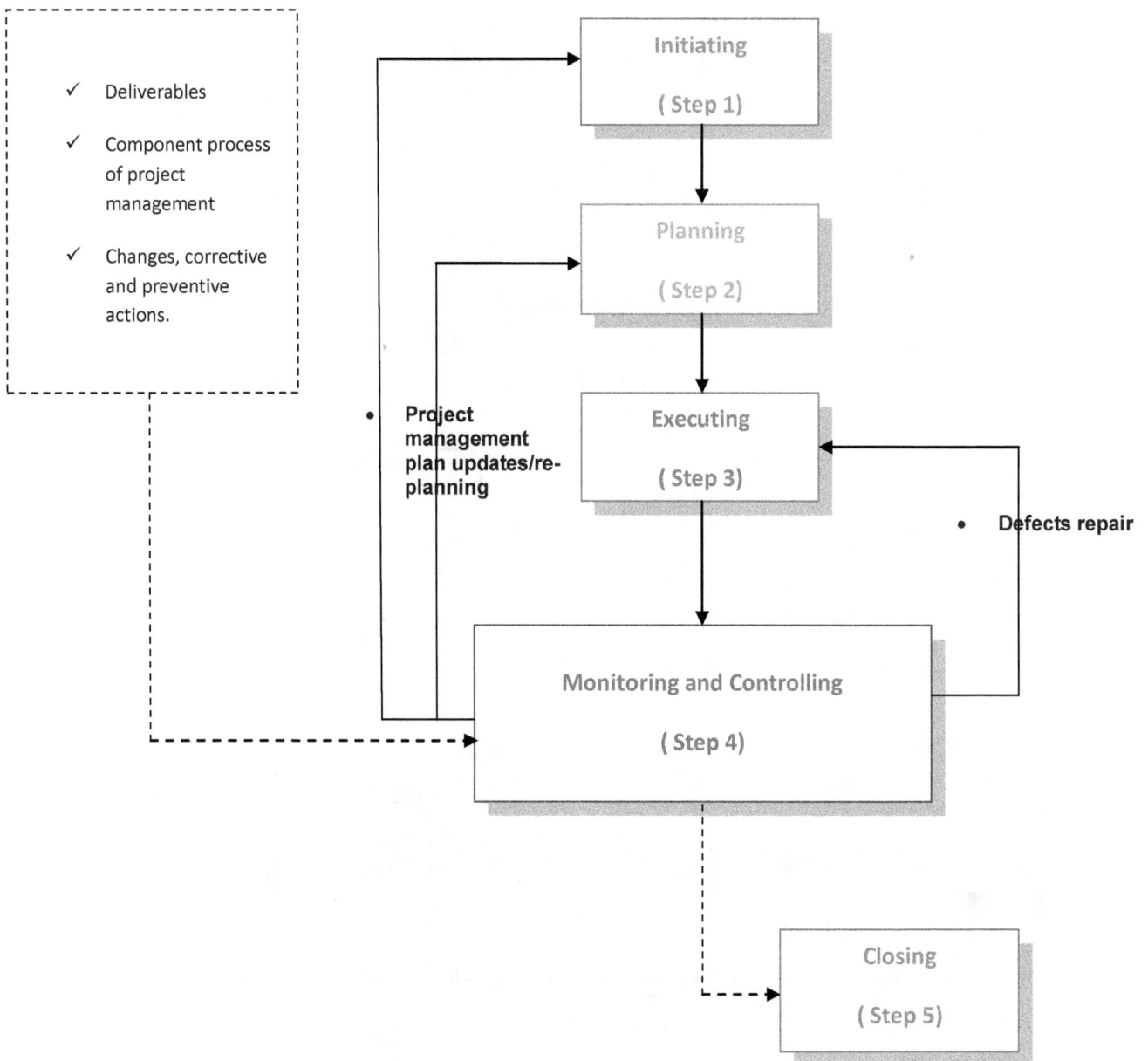

```
┌───────────────────────┐                    ┌──────────────────┐
│                       │                    │    Initiating    │
│  ✓  Deliverables      │                    │                  │
│                       │                    │    ( Step 1)     │
│  ✓  Component process │                    └──────────────────┘
│     of project        │                             │
│     management        │                             ▼
│                       │                    ┌──────────────────┐
│  ✓  Changes, corrective│                   │     Planning     │
│     and preventive    │                    │                  │
│     actions.          │                    │    ( Step 2)     │
│                       │                    └──────────────────┘
└───────────────────────┘                             │
                                                       ▼
                          • Project            ┌──────────────────┐
                            management         │    Executing     │
                            plan updates/re-   │                  │
                            planning           │    ( Step 3)     │
                                               └──────────────────┘
                                                                  • Defects repair
                                               ┌──────────────────────────────┐
                                               │  Monitoring and Controlling  │
                                               │                              │
                                               │          ( Step 4)           │
                                               └──────────────────────────────┘
                                                              │
                                                              ▼
                                                     ┌──────────────────┐
                                                     │     Closing      │
                                                     │                  │
                                                     │    ( Step 5)     │
                                                     └──────────────────┘
```

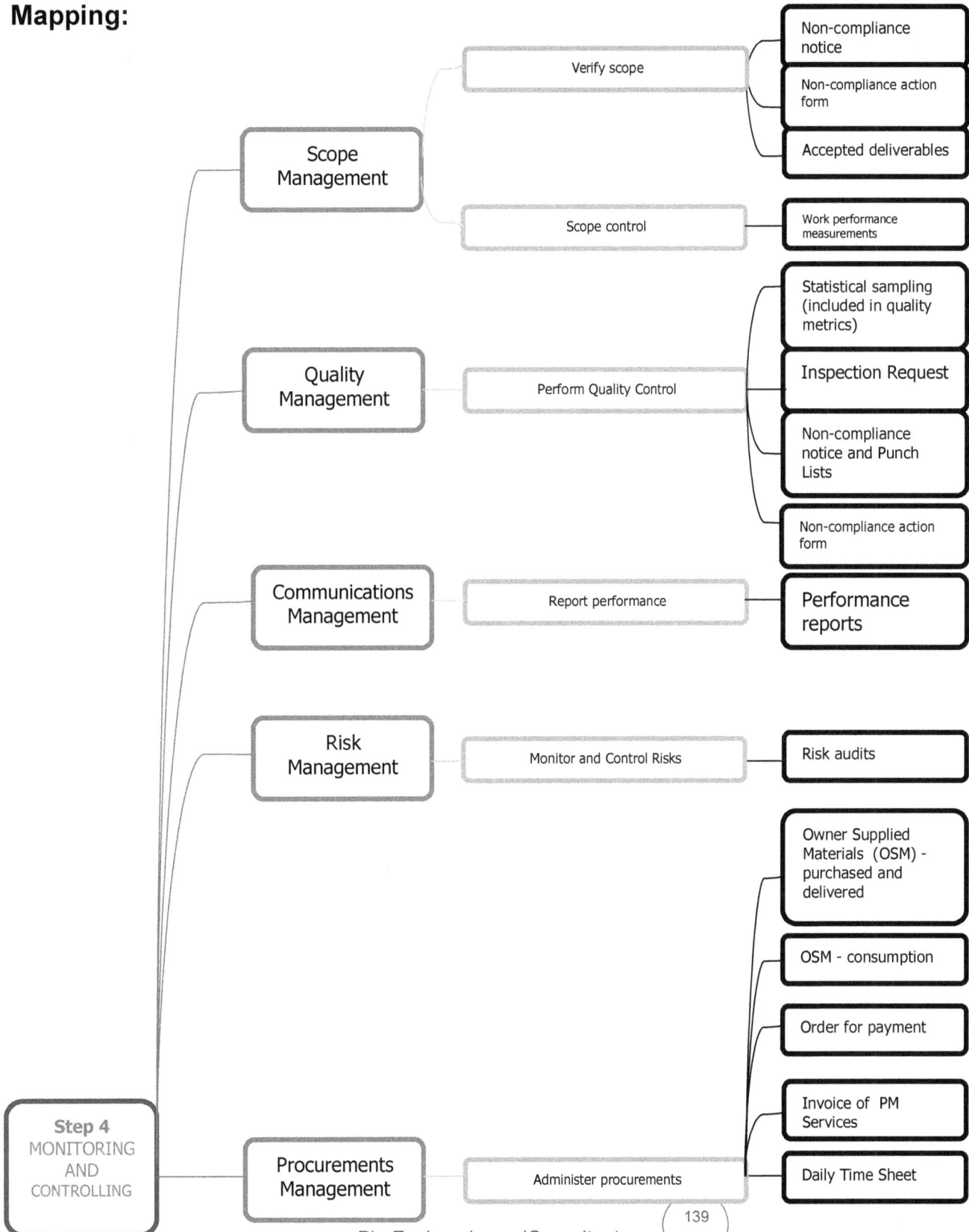

Mapping:

	Verify scope	Non-compliance notice
		Non-compliance action form
Scope Management		Accepted deliverables
	Scope control	Work performance measurements
		Statistical sampling (included in quality metrics)
Quality Management	Perform Quality Control	Inspection Request
		Non-compliance notice and Punch Lists
		Non-compliance action form
Communications Management	Report performance	Performance reports
Risk Management	Monitor and Control Risks	Risk audits
		Owner Supplied Materials (OSM) - purchased and delivered
		OSM - consumption
		Order for payment
		Invoice of PM Services
Procurements Management	Administer procurements	Daily Time Sheet

Step 4
MONITORING AND CONTROLLING

139

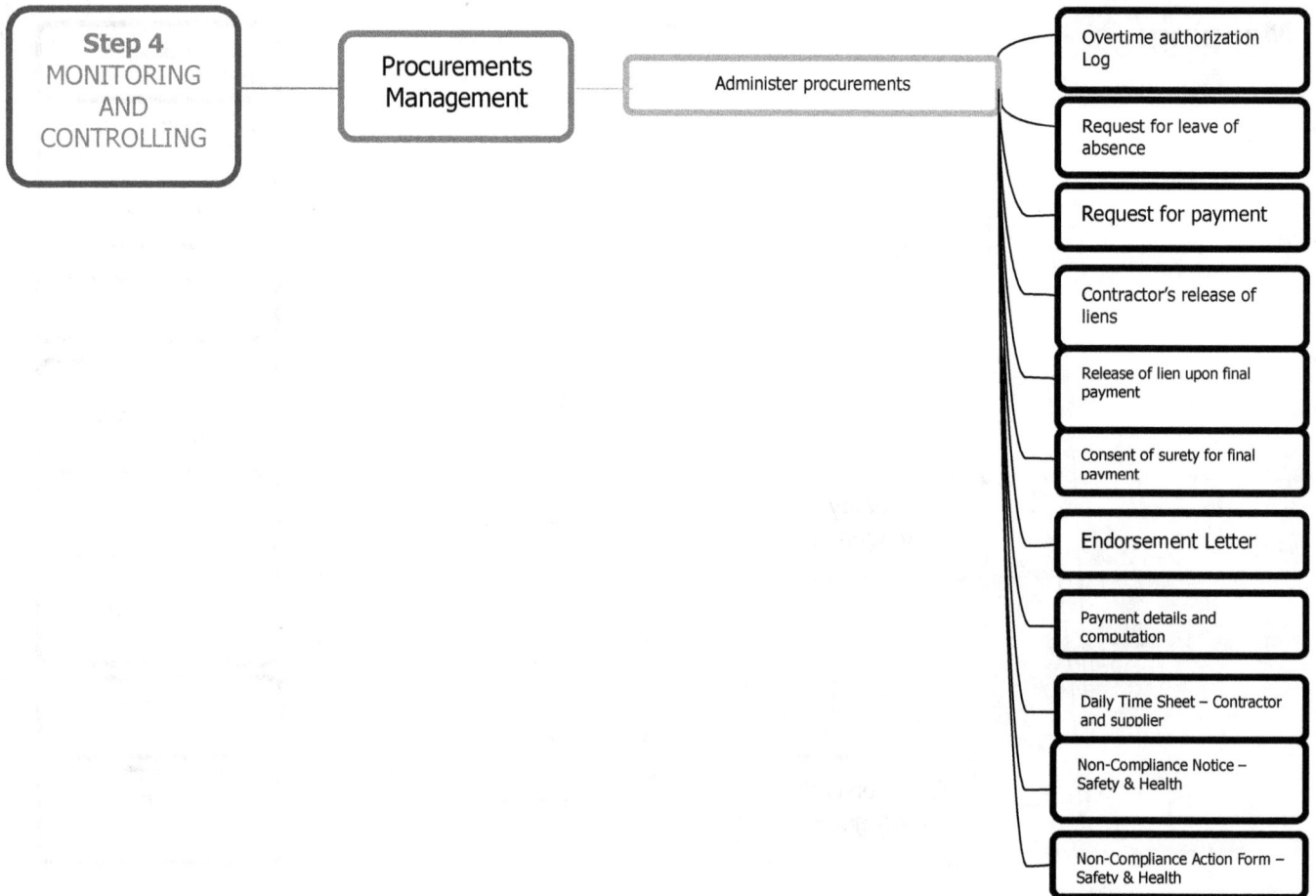

ACCEPTED DELIVERABLES

Is a list or summary of deliverables that has been approved. All deliverables that complied with the specified requirements and/or acceptance criteria are to be approved and signed off by the customer or sponsor. This document is being done during the fourth step of managing projects.

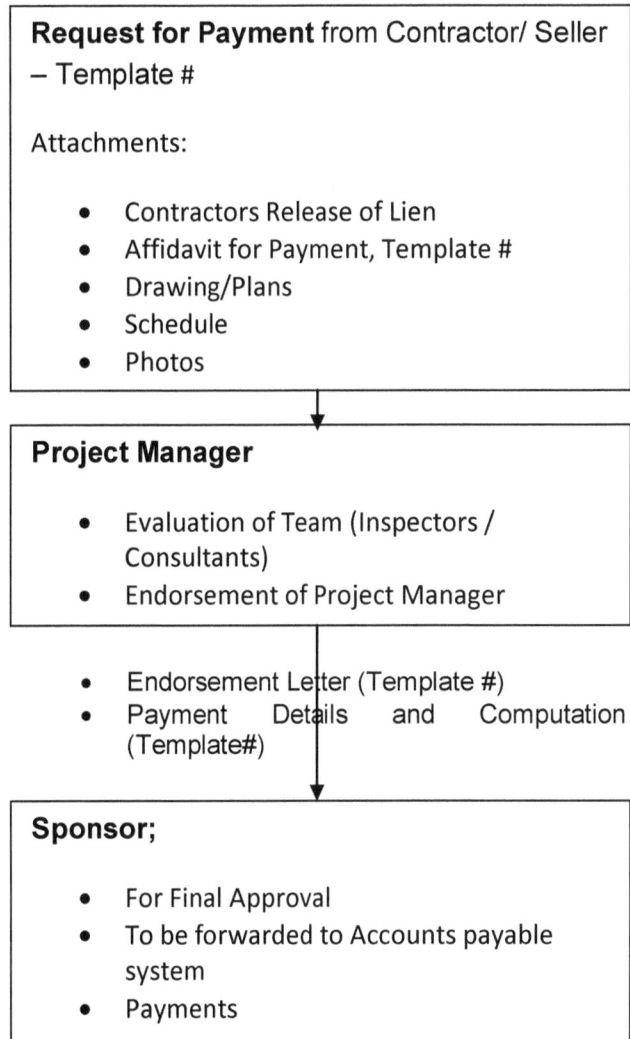

Templates : Inspection- Non Compliance Notice (NCN), Inspection- Non Compliance Action (NCA), Accepted Deliverables

WORK PERFORMANCE MEASUREMENTS

Work performance measurements refer to the metrics of the project activity that is established to evaluate the actual progress of the project versus the planned progress. It covers the evaluation of scope, time, cost, and quality of the project. This document is being done during the fourth step of managing projects.

Templates : Work Performance Measurements, Statistical Sampling, Inspection Request, Inspection-Non Compliance Notice (NCN), Punch Lists, Inspection-Non Compliance Action (NCA)

PERFORMANCE REPORT

Performance report illustrates the overall progress or result of the project. It is collected progressively and ought to be sent to stakeholders as part of communication process. The information that needs to be communicated includes the project status, its progress, and performance measurement for cost, schedule, scope, and quality. This document is often done during the fourth step of managing projects.

Templates : Performance Report, Risk Audit, Owner Supplied Materials-Purchased, Owner Supplied Materials-Consumption.

PAYMENT SYSTEM

A payment system dictates the payment process that the buyer needs to accomplish, according to the completed work or delivered items of the authorized person on the team. The system is capable of verifying these data, checking the requirements, and authenticating the contract provisions prior to submission to accounts department for payment process. This document is being done during the fourth step of managing projects.

Request for Payment from Contractor/ Seller – Template #

Attachments:

- Contractors Release of Lien
- Affidavit for Payment, Template #
- Drawing/Plans
- Schedule
- Photos

Project Manager

- Evaluation of Team (Inspectors / Consultants)
- Endorsement of Project Manager

- Endorsement Letter (Template #)
- Payment Details and Computation (Template#)

Sponsor;

- For Final Approval
- To be forwarded to Accounts payable system
- Payments

Templates : Order For Payment

Templates : Invoice of PM Services, Daily Time Sheet, Overtime Authorization Log, Request For Leave, Request For Payment, Contractor's Release of Lien, Release of Lien upon final payment, Consent of surety for final payment, Endorsement Letter, Payment details and computation, Daily time sheet –seller , Non-compliance notice –Safety & Health (*Use for construction project*) , Non-compliance Action Form –Safety & Health (*Use for construction project*).

Company Address :
Telephone :
Fax :
Email : info@
Website : www.

Non Compliance Notice (NCN)

		Date Prepared: 02/28/15	Template ID: MCT-SC-001
Project	Name of the Project	**Revision:** 000	**Pages :** 1 of 1
Project Package	Name of the package / phase of the project		
Project Location	Name of the location of the project	**Reference No. :** CM-PEC-D-0066-2015	

Contractor's/Seller's Company Name Company A	**Contractor's/Seller's Name : In charge** Engineer X **Role :** Construction Manager
WBS ID:	**Scope / Work Package / Requirement:** Retaining Wall	**Reference :**(Drawing , Specification , Contract provision etc.)

No.	Description	Structure location/ Particular	Current Status / Condition
1	**Total number** of vertical Reinforcement	Retaining Wall at Grid line 1 and Grid line D-G	Installation of reinforcement steel bar

Issued by ;

_____
QC / Inspector

Received by ;

_____
Contractor / Seller

Noted by ;

_____
Project Manager

Date Received ;

_____

Company Address :
Telephone :
Fax :
Email : info@
Website : www.

Non Compliance Action Form

		Date Prepared: 02/28/15	Template ID: MCT-SC-002
Project	Name of the Project	**Revision :** 000	**Pages:** 1 of 1
Project Package	Name of the package / phase of the project		
Project Location	Name of the location of the project	**Reference No. :** CM-PEC-D-0067-2015	

Contractor's/Seller's Company Name Company A	**Contractor's/Seller's Name : In charge** Engineer X **Role :** Project Manager
WBS ID : **Scope / Work Package / Requirement:** Retaining Wall	**Reference :** (Drawing , Specification , Contract provision etc.)

Corrective Action / Defect Repair

No.	Description	Action	Date of Completion	Inspector / Consultant's Comment
1	**Total number** of vertical Reinforcement	Re work and corrected as per specified total number of bars		

Certified by ;

_____ / Date _____
Contractor's Quality Control

Verified by ;

_____ / Date _____
Contractor's Project Manager

Received / Approved ;

_____ / Date _____
Inspector / Consultant

Noted by ;

_____ / Date _____
Project Manager

Your Logo here!

Accepted Deliverables

		Date Prepared : 02/28/15	Template ID: MCT-SC-003
Project	Name of the Project	Revision : 000	Pages : 1 of 1
Project Package	Name of the package / phase of the project	Reference No. : CM-PEC-D-0068-2015	
Project Location	Name of the location of the project		

ID	Category	Deliverables	Requirements			Status	Acceptance
			Specified	Acceptance Criteria	Reference	Verification		

www.ConstructionProjectManagementPro.com

Work Performance Measurements

Company Address :
Telephone :
Fax :
Email : info@
Website : www.

Template ID:	MCT-SC-004
Pages :	1 of 2

Project	Name of the Project
Project Package	Name of the package / phase of the project
Project Location	Name of the location of the project

Date Prepared :	02/28/15
Revision :	000
Reference No. :	CM-PEC-D-0069-2015

ID	Category	Deliverable

Schedule

Value	Interpretation
SV	✓
SPI	✓

Cost

Value	Interpretation
CV	✓
CPI	✓

Scope
(scope / technical performance)

Quality
(technical performance)

Schedule

Value	Interpretation
SV	✓
SPI	✓

Cost

Value	Interpretation
CV	✓
CPI	✓

Scope
(scope / technical performance)

Quality
(technical performance)

Company Address :
Telephone :
Fax :
Email - info@
Website :: www.

Your Logo here!

Work Performance Measurements

Date Issue :	02/28/15	Pages :	2 of 2
Reference No. :	CM-PEC-D-0069-2013		
Revision No. :	000		

ID	Category	Deliverable	Schedule		Cost		Scope (scope / technical performance)	Quality (technical performance)
			Value	**Interpretation**	**Value**	**Interpretation**		
			SV		CV			
			SPI		CPI			
			Value	**Interpretation**	**Value**	**Interpretation**		
			SV		CV			
			SPI		CPI			

Statistical Sampling

		Template ID: MCT-Q-001
Project	Name of the Project	**Date Prepared :** 02/28/15
Project Package	Fire Protection, Plumbing, HVAC, Electrical, Testing and Commissioning	**Revision :** 000 **Pages :** 1 of 1
Project Location	Name of the location of the project	**Reference No. :** CM-PEC-D-0070-2015

ID	Category	Item	Description	Method of Measurements	Metrics	Reference	Statistical Sampling
PP-01	Bored Pile	Concrete	Cast in place concrete pile (bored pile)	Compressive Test	3,000 psi (@28 days)	Structural Plan	• 5 Sets of cylinder at 3 piles / day
				Slump	100mm (max.)	Structural Plan / Structural Specification	• For each batch of concrete • 6 cu.m which ever is lesser
		Reinforcing Steel	Bored pile reinforcing steel	Tensile (Fy) 12mm dia. Bar and larger	413.7Mpa (60 ksi)		2.5 Tons per diameter per kind
				10mm dia bar And smaller	276 Mpa (40 ksi)		2.5 Tons per diameter per kind
				Bending	No Crack		2.5 Tons per diameter per kind
PP-02e	Concrete Works , supply, fabrication, delivery and erection	Reinforcing Steel	Reinforcing Steel	Tensile (Fy) 12mm dia. Bar and larger	413.7Mpa (60 ksi)	Structural Plan / Structural Specification	2.5 Tons per diameter per kind
				10mm dia bar And smaller	276 Mpa (40 ksi)		2.5 Tons per diameter per kind
				Bending	No Crack		2.5 Tons per diameter per kind

	Inspection Request		Date Prepared : 02/28/15	Template ID: MCT-Q-002
Project	Name of the Project		**Revision :** 000	**Pages :** 1 of 1
Project Location	Name of the location of the project		**Reference No. :** CM-PEC-D-0071-2015	

Company Address :
Telephone :
Fax :
Email : info@
Website : www.

Contractor's/Seller's Company Name : Company A	Prepared by : Engineer X	Request No. 1

Mark applicable item below

Architectural	Structural	
Electrical	Mechanical	
Fire Protection Works	Others	

Description :

Received by(Inspector/Consultant) :	Inspection	
	Date:	**Time:**

Instruction / Comments :

Inspected/Commented by :	**Forwarded/ Received by(Contractor/Seller):**
Name and Signature: Role Company Date	Name and Signature of Seller/Contractor : Role Company Date

Non Compliance Notice (NCN)

Company Address :
Telephone :
Fax :
Email : info@
Website : www.

		Date Prepared: 02/28/15	Template ID: MCT-Q-003
Project	Name of the Project	**Revision :** 000	**Pages :** 1 of 1
Project Package	Name of the package / phase of the project		
Project Location	Name of the location of the project	**Reference No. :** CM-PEC-D-0072-2015	

Contractor's/Seller's Company Name Company A	**Contractor's/Seller's Name: In charge** Engineer X **Role :**Project Manager
WBS ID:	**Scope / Work Package / Requirement:** Retaining Wall	**Reference :**(Drawing , Specification, Contract provision etc.)

No.	Description	Structure location /Particular	Current Status / Condition
1	Spacing of vertical Reinforcement	Retaining Wall at Grid line 1 and Grid line D-G	Installation of reinforcement steel bar

Issued by ;

_____
QC / Inspector

Noted by ;

_____
Project Manager

Received by ;

_____
Contractor / Seller

Date Received ;

_____

Your Logo here!

Punch Lists

		Date Prepared : 02/28/15	Template ID: MCT-Q-003a
Project	Name of the Project	Revision : 000	Pages : 1 of 1
Project Package	Name of the package / phase of the project		
Project Location	Name of the location of the project	Reference No.: CM-PEC-D-0095-2015	

Punch Lists

Item No.	Category	Deliverables	Area/Location	Description	Action	Date			Status	Remarks
						Issued	Closure			
							Target	Actual		
1	Architectural	Ceiling	4th Floor, Room 401	Bottom of beam and slab – Shrinkage Cracks	Apply **Brand** Coat for all cracks				Still on progress	Ongoing application of coats . 80% done

Prepared by : **Inspector**

Noted by : **Consultant**

Non Compliance Action Form

		Date Prepared: 02/28/15	Template ID: MCT-Q-004
Project	Name of the Project	**Revision:** 000	**Pages:** 1 of 1
Project Package	Name of the package / phase of the project		
Project Location	Name of the location of the project	**Reference No. :** CM-PEC-D-0073-2015	

Contractor's/Seller's Company Name Company A	**Contractor's/Seller's Name : In charge** Engineer X **Role :** Project Manager
WBS ID : **Scope / Work Package / Requirement:** Retaining Wall	**Reference :** (Drawing , Specification , Contract provision etc.)

Corrective Action / Defect Repair

No.	Description	Action	Date of Completion	Inspector / Consultant's Comment
1	Spacing of vertical Reinforcement	Re work and corrected as per specified spacing		

Certified by ;

_____ / Date
Contractor's Quality Control

Verified by ;

_____ / Date
Contractor's Project Manager

Received / Approved ;

_____ / Date
Inspector / Consultant

Noted by ;

_____ / Date
Project Manager

Performance Report

		Date Prepared : 02/28/15	Template ID: MCT-COM-001
		Revision : 000	Pages : 1 of 4
Project	Name of the Project		
Project Package	Name of the package / phase of the project	Reference No. : CM-PEG-R-0009-2015	
Project Location	Name of the location of the project		

PROGRESS – (Over all Work Accomplished)

You can plot the schedule in terms of bar chart with as planned vs. actual accomplishment.

WBS ID	Task Name	Duration	Start	Finish
1	- Bored Piling Project	56 days?	Thu 4/25/13	Thu 7/11/13
1.1	- General Requirements	47 days	Thu 4/25/13	Fri 6/28/13
1.1.1	Mobilization	13 days	Thu 4/25/13	Mon 5/13/13
1.1.2	Temporary Facilities installation/erection	21 days	Thu 4/25/13	Thu 5/23/13
1.1.3	Material Handling and logistics	42 days	Thu 5/2/13	Fri 6/28/13
1.1.4	Demobilization	14 days	Mon 6/10/13	Thu 6/27/13
1.2	- Earth Works	47 days	Thu 4/25/13	Fri 6/28/13
1.2.1	Trimming and clearing	43 days	Thu 4/25/13	Fri 6/28/13
1.2.2	Hauling of excavated and cleared materials	14 days	Tue 4/30/13	Fri 5/17/13
1.3	- Load Bearing and Foundation Works	56 days	Thu 4/25/13	Thu 7/11/13
1.3.1	Steel casing fabrication	21 days	Thu 4/25/13	Thu 5/23/13
1.3.2	Bored Piling	35 days	Thu 5/2/13	Wed 6/19/13
1.3.3	Top of Pile cutting off	21 days	Wed 5/22/13	Wed 6/19/13
1.3.4	Fabrication of Rebar Case	35 days	Fri 5/24/13	Thu 7/11/13
1.3.5	Survey and Lay outing	35 days	Fri 5/24/13	Thu 7/11/13
1.4	Sign off	1 day?	Thu 7/11/13	Thu 7/11/13

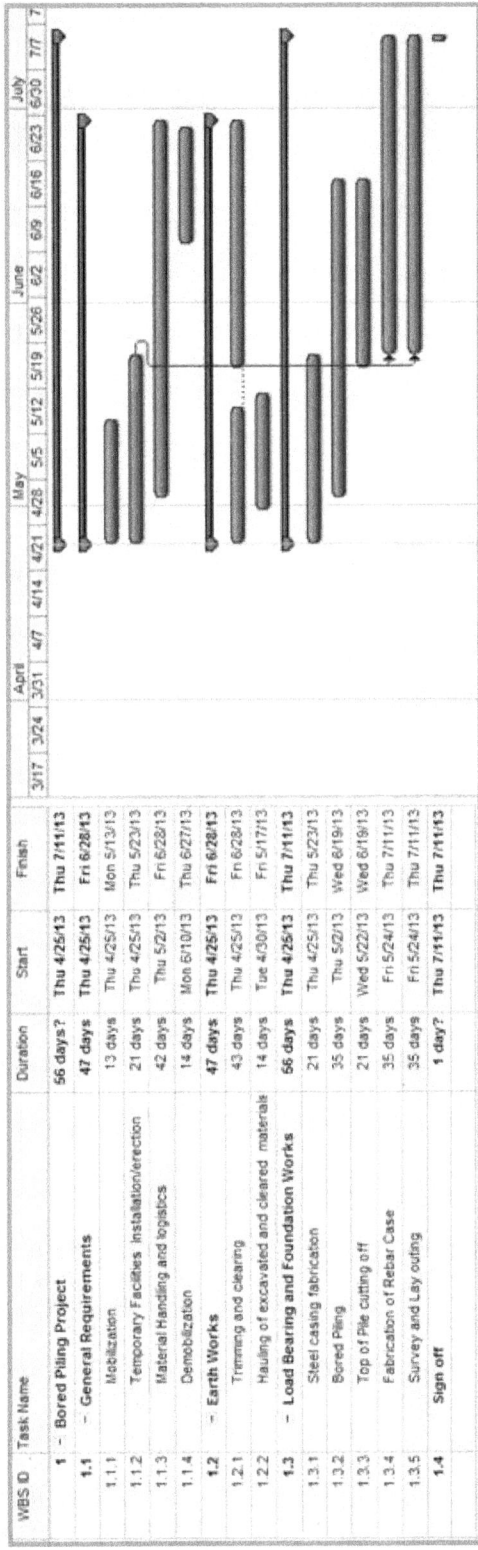

This illustration , Lists is for illustrative only and not intended to portray any construction projects , scope ,description or not representing any specific ways to organize , plan of any type of construction projects

www.ConstructionProjectManagementPro.com

Company Address :
Telephone :
Fax :
Email : info@
Website : www.

Pages :
2 of 4

Performance Report

| Date Issue : 02/28/15 |
| Reference No. : CM-PEC-R-0009-2015 |
| Revision No. : 000 |

STATUS – (stands on performance measurement baseline)

SCHEDULE

WBS ID	Work Package / Description	Planned %	Actual %	Variance	Status
1.1	General Requirements				
1.2	Mobilization / Demobilization				
1.3	Bored Pile	9.94	0.13	- 9.81	19 Calendar days behind the schedule
1.4	Excavation/ Backfill				
1.5	Masonry				
1.6	Structural Steel				
1.6.1	Fabrication				
1.6.2	Erection				
1.7	Architectural				
1.8	Electrical				

This illustration , Lists is for illustrative only and not intended to portray any construction projects , scope ,description or not representing any specific ways to organize , plan of any type of construction projects

Performance Report

COST :

(You can use also the plot of schedule with s-curve)

WBS ID	Work Package / Description	Planned %	Actual %	Variance	Status
1.1	General Requirements				
1.2	Mobilization / Demobilization				
1.3	Bored Pile				
1.4	Excavation/ Backfill				
1.5	Masonry				
1.6	Structural Steel				
1.6.1	Fabrication				
1.6.2	Erection				
1.7	Architectural				
1.8	Electrical				

This illustration , Lists is for illustrative only and not intended to portray any construction projects , scope ,description or not representing any specific ways to organize , plan of any type of construction projects.

Your Logo here!

Performance Report

Company Address :
Telephone :
Fax :
Email : info@
Website : www.

Date Issue : 02/28/15
Reference No. : CM-PEC-R-0009-2015
Revision No. : 000
Pages : 4 of 4

RISKS AND ISSUES – (stands on performance measurement baseline)

Risk	Status

Issue	Status

www.ConstructionProjectManagementPro.com

Company Address :
Telephone :
Fax :
Email : info@
Website : www.

Risk Audit

		Date Prepared : 02/28/15	**Template ID:** MCT-R-001
Project	Name of the Project	**Revision :** 000	**Pages :** 1 of 1
Project Package	Name of the package / phase of the project		
Project Location	Name of the location of the project	**Reference No. :** CM-PEC-D-0074-2015	

Risks

No.	Risks	Root Cause	Response Description	Remarks

Response

	Response improvements	Remarks

Risk Management Process

Process	Techniques	Process Improvements	Remarks

Owner Supplied Materials(OSM) Purchased and Delivered

Company Address :
Telephone :
Fax :
Email : info@
Website : www.

Template ID:
MCT-P-001

Date Prepared :
02/28/15

Pages :
1 of 1

Revision :
000

Reference No.:
CM-PEC-D-0075-2015

Project	Name of the Project
Project Package	Name of the package / phase of the project
Project Location	Name of the location of the project

No.	Description	Manufacturer /Supplier	Date		Quantity		Unit	Contract Reference	Status
			Material Request	Delivery	Total	Delivered			

Company Address :
Telephone :
Fax :
Email : info@
Website : www.

Owner Supplied Materials (OSM) - Consumption

Project	Name of the Project
Project Package	Name of the package / phase of the project
Project Location	Name of the location of the project

Date Prepared : 02/28/15	Template ID: MCT-P-0002
Revision : 000	Pages : 1 of 1
Reference No. :	

CM-PEC-D-0076-2015

No.	Description	Seller / Supplier	Quantity			Consumption			Balance as of date	Status
			Total	Delivered	Previous	This Period	Total as of date			

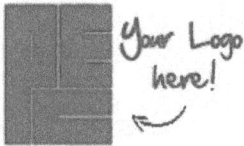

Template ID: MCP-P-003
Revision: 000

Reference No. : CM-PEC-D-0077-2015

Date: February 28, 2015
Page 1 of 1

ORDER FOR PAYMENT

ATTENTION : Name in charge / Owners Representative for Accounts
Accounting/Administrative Division

PARTICULARS :

We hereby recommend the release of payment of **Supplier's Name,**
 Supplier's Company Name , for the items/materials delivered on site
and to be used for ***specify the work package/ particular work.***

Project :			**Date Prepared :**
Project Package :			
Project Location :			
ITEM	**DESCRIPTION**	**AMOUNT**	**COMMENTS**

Attachment;
   ✓ Delivery Receipts
   ✓ Invoice
   ✓ Others

Checked by: Authorized by:

_____   _____

Site Personnel/ Inspector   **Project Manager**

Approved by:

_____

Sponsor /Customer

Company Address:
Tel :0000000
Fax : 0000000
Email : info@
Website: www

Template ID: MCT-P-004
Revision: 000
Page 1 of 1

BILLING INVOICE

SPONSOR / CUSTOMER DETAILS		Invoice Date :	Due Date : 30 days only
SOLD TO : Sponsor's / Customers' Company Name		**Invoice No. :**	**Payment/Billing No.**
ADDRESS : Project Location		**Project Code :**	**Contract No / Reference :**
ATTENTION : Sponsor's Name or Owner's Representative			

DESCRIPTION OF SERVICES	AMOUNT
Project Management Services for the ***Proposed Name of the Project*** Located at ***Location of the project/ Address***. Contract Reference No._____ Dated , ***contract date*** Contract Amount $_____ Services for the period of Month/ Day - Month/Day ,Year	

Prepared by : **Accountant**	**TOTAL SALE**	
Verified / Reviewed by: **Accounting Manager**	**VAT**	
Approved by: **Project Manager**	**AMOUNT DUE**	$

Company Address :
Telephone :
Fax :
Email : info@
Website : www. .

Daily Time Sheet

Date Prepared: 02/28/15	Template ID: MCT-P-005	

Project	Name of the Project	**Revision :** 000	**Pages :** 1 of 1
Project Package	Name of the package / phase of the project		
Project Location	Name of the location of the project	**Reference No. :** CM-PEC-D-0079-2015	

Name	Regular Time (Reg)				Over Time (OT)		
	Time In	Signature	Time Out	Signature	Time In	Time Out	Signature

Certified by:

Noted by:

_____

Name / Signature
Site Administrative Officer

_____

Name/Signature
Project Manager

Company Address :
Telephone :
Fax :
Email : info@
Website : www.

Overtime Authorization Log

Date Prepared: 02/28/15	**Template ID:** MCT-P-006		

Project	Name of the Project	**Revision :** 000	**Pages :** 1 of 1
Project Package	Name of the package / phase of the project		
Project Location	Name of the location of the project	**Reference No. :** CM-PEC-D-0080-2015	

Name	Overtime Hours			Remarks
	Time In	Time Out	Total hours	

Authorized by: Noted by:

_____   _____

Name / Signature   **Name/Signature**
Construction Manager   Project Manager

Company Address :
Telephone :
Fax :
Email : info@
Website : www.

Request for Leave of Absence

		Date Prepared: 02/28/15	Template ID: MCT-P-007
Project	Name of the Project	**Revision:** 000	**Pages :** 1 of 1
Project Package	Name of the package / phase of the project		
Project Location	Name of the location of the project	**Reference No. :** CM-PEC-D-0081-2015	

Requested by :		**Employee Number :**	
		Division / Department :	
Nature of leave		( ) Sick	( ) Vacation
		( ) Emergency	( ) Maternity
		( ) Paternity	( ) Others
Period of leave		From:	To:
Days/Hours		Number of Days:	Equivalent Hours:

Reason for leave:

Approved by:

_____
Site Staff Signature :

_____
Project Manager:

Human Resource Department (HRD) Verification	Type of leave	Available	Required	Balance
	sick			
	vacation			
	emergency			
	maternity			
	paternity			
	Others			

_____
Human Resource Officer

Your LOGO Here! – Contractor

Company Address:
Tel :0000000
Fax : 0000000
Email : info@
Website: www

Template ID: MCT-P-008
Revision: 000

Reference No. : CM-PEC-D-0082-2015

| Attention | : | **PROJECT MANAGER'S NAME** |
| | | Organization / Company Name |

| Project | : | **NAME OF THE PROJECT** |

| Project Package | : | PP 01 – General Civil and Architectural Works |

| Location | : | Project Location |

| Subject | : | **PROGRESS BILLING NUMBER 1** *(Generally, Construction Projects Have progress billings or a monthly billing based on their Accomplishments).* |

Dear Sir,

Relative to the above project , we hereby request payment for the works completed covering periods from *month /day – month / day, year* with our accomplishment equivalent to **state percent** *(example 4.5 %)* amounting to **AMOUNT IN WORDS ($ - AMOUNT IN FIGURES).**

Attached here with are, site photo graphs, detailed computation of accomplishment, drawings or plans that shown portion of accomplished works.

If you have any clarifications, please advise us.

Respectfully Yours,

Signature:

Name of the Seller / Contractor
Role

Organization or Company Name

Your LOGO Here! – Contractor

Company Address:
Tel :0000000
Fax : 0000000
Email : info@
Website: www

Template ID: MCT-P-009
Revision: 000

Reference No.: CM-PEC-D-0083-2015

Date: February 28, 2015
Page 1 of 1

CONTRACTOR'S COMPANY NAME
Address

RELEASE OF LIENS

To All Whom it May Concern:

For valuable consideration, the undersigned has been hired as a CONTRACTOR by **PROJECT SPONSOR/CUSTOMER** to render all labor, materials, equipment and services for **Project Name, Project Package,** located at Project location and address.

NOW THEREFORE, this **2ⁿᵈday of May**(Month) ,**2013** (year), the undersigned hereby releases the property of the **PROJECT SPONSOR/CUSTOMER**, located at Project location and address,

From any liability from lien for all labor, materials, equipment and services rendered and or delivered for that said property.

CONTRACTOR'S COMPANY NAME
Contractor

_____
Authorized Representative Signature

_____
Name
Role

"This Release of Lien Template/Form is for illustrative only , Consult your legal adviser or attorney for further details."

Your LOGO Here!

Company Address:
Tel:0000000
Fax: 0000000
Email: info@
Website: www

Template ID: MCT-P-010
Revision: 000

Reference No. : CM-PEC-D-0084-2015

Date: February 28, 2015
Page 1 of 1

CONTRACTOR'S COMPANY NAME
Address

CONTRACTOR'S RELEASE OF LIENS UPON FINAL PAYMENT

To All Whom it May Concern:

For valuable consideration, the undersigned has been hired as a CONTRACTOR by **PROJECT SPONSOR/CUSTOMER** to render all labor, materials, equipment and services for **Project Name, Project Package ,**located at Project location and address .

NOW THEREFORE, this **2nd day of May**(Month) ,**2013** (year) , upon the receipt of the undersigned for and in consideration of the final amount from **PROJECT SPONSOR/CUSTOMER** the sum of $_____ as final payment, does hereby waive and release any lien rights the undersigned has on the property of **PROJECT SPONSOR/CUSTOMER NAME**, located at Project location.

CONTRACTOR'S COMPANY NAME
Contractor

_____
Authorized Representative Signature

_____
Name
Role

"This Release of Lien Template/Form is for illustrative only, Consult your legal adviser or attorney for further details."

Your LOGO Here!

Company Address:
Tel:0000000
Fax: 0000000
Email: info@
Website: www

Template ID: MCT-P-011
Revision: 000

Reference No. : CM-PEC-D-0085-2015

Date: February 28, 2015
Page 1 of 1

SURETY   COMPANY NAME
Address

CONSENT OF SURETY UPON FINAL PAYMENT

Project   :   P.E.C. School Building Project – *(Project Name)*
Project Package   :
Project Location   :

In consideration of the contract made between the Contractor and the Sponsor/Customer, the surety company, **SURETY   COMPANY NAME, ADDRESS,BRANCH)** on the Payment Bond of the Contractor, **CONTRACTOR'S NAME, ADDRESS,** is hereby approves the issuance of final payment, said final payment does not relieve the surety company to its obligation to the Sponsor / Customer, **NAME OF THE SPONSOR/CUSTOMER, ADDRESS**

IN WITNESS WHERE OF, We have set our hands this **21ˢᵗday** of **May** (month), **2013**(year).

SURETY COMPANY NAME

By:

_____   _____
Name   **Name**
Branch Manager   Senior Manager

"This Consent Surety Template/Form is for illustrative only, Consult a surety company near you for details

PIER ENGINEERING and CONSULTANTS

Project Managers • Consulting Engineers

Company Address:
Tel :0000000
Fax : 0000000
Email : info@
Website: www

Template ID: MCT-P-012
Revision: 000

Reference No. : CM-PEC-L-0004-2015

Date: February 28, 2015
Page 1 of 1

SPONSOR'S / CUSTOMER'S COMPANY NAME

Address

Attention	:	**PROJECT SPONSOR/ CUSTOMER'S NAME**
Project	:	**NAME OF THE PROJECT**
Project Package	:	PP 01 – General Civil and Architectural Works
Location	:	Project Location
Subject	:	**RECOMMENDATION FOR PROGRESS BILLING No. 01**
Contractor /Seller	:	**CONTRACTOR / SELLER'S COMPANY NAME**

Gentlemen :

We recommend herewith, for your approval, the request for first progress payment of **Contractor's / Seller's Company Name** for the *Project Package* of the *Project Name* . We have evaluated the request and hereby recommend payment in the total amount of **USD:*AMOUNT IN WORDS* ($ - Amount if figures)**representing *percentage %(example 4.5%)* of the work accomplishment.

Attached are the billing request of **CONTRACTOR /SELLER'S COMPANY NAME** dated *state the date of request for payment letter of contractor / seller*, the evaluated accomplishment report as of *date where the evaluation report was made.*

Trusting you will find the above in order.

Very truly yours   Noted by:

_____   _____
Construction Manager   Project Manager

169

Company Address:
Tel :0000000
Fax : 0000000
Email : info@
Website: www

Template ID: MCT-P-013
Revision: 000

Reference No.: CM-PEC-D-0086-2015

PAYMENT DETAILS AND COMPUTATION

This is to certify that in accordance with the terms and conditions of the contract executed on *Date and Year of the contract (Day 1)* by and between (OWNER*) Name of the Sponsor* and (CONTRACTOR) *the company name of the Contractor/ Seller* for the *Project Package Name* of the **PROPOSED** *NAME OF THE PROJECT*, located at Project location.

There will be due and payable from the Owner to the Contractor the sum of USD : **AMOUNT IN WORDS**		**H**
1. Contract Amount	A	
2. Additions / Deductions (impact from changes)		
Change Order No. 01	B	
3. Contract Amount to date(with effect of changes)	C	
4. Value of Work completed to date, 10.498%		D
5. Less:		
a. Retention 10%	10% of Contract Amount , verify contract condition	
b. Repayment of downpayment,	pro rate the value of dow n payment w ith total dproject duration	
Sub-Total (Deductions)		E
6. Total amount due to Contractor		F
7. Less: Previous Progress Payment	G	
8. Amount due to Contract Now		H
9. Contract Balance including Retention		I
10. Summary of Payments	J+G+H	
10.1 Advance Payment	J	
10.2 First Progress Billing	G	
10.3 Second Progress Billing (This Billing)	H	

EVALUATED PERCENTAGE OF WORK COMPLETED TO DATE: ___%

CERTIFIED CORRECT BY: NOTED ;

NAME   **PROJECT MANAGER'S NAME**
Construction Manager   Project Manager

Company Address :
Telephone :
Fax :
Email : info@
Website : www.

Daily Time Sheet - Seller

Date Prepared: 02/28/15		**Template ID:** MCT-P-014	

Project	Name of the Project	**Revision :** 000	**Pages :** 1 of 1
Project Package	Name of the package / phase of the project		
Project Location	Name of the location of the project	**Reference No. :** CM-PEC-D-087-2015	

Name	Regular Time (Reg)				Over Time (OT)		
	Time In	Signature	Time Out	Signature	Time In	Time Out	Signature

Certified by:

Noted by:

_____

Name / Signature
Site Administrative Officer

_____

Name/Signature
Project Manager

Your Logo here!

Non Compliance Notice (NCN) - Safety and Health

		Date Prepared: 02/28/15	Template ID: MCT-EHS-001
Project	Name of the Project	**Revision :** 000	**Pages :** 1 of 1
Project Package	Name of the package / phase of the project		
Project Location	Name of the location of the project	**Reference No. :** CM-PEC-D-0046-2015	

Contractor's/Seller's Company Name Company A	Contractor's/Seller's Name : In charge Engineer X Role :Project Manager

NOTICE NO. 001	Scope / Work Package / Requirement:	Reference :(Contract provision and others)

Description	Specific location (Working Area)	Due Date
Safety:		
Hard Hat		
Safety shoes		
Rain Gear		
Gloves		
Goggles/Safety Glasses		
Safety Full Body Harness		
Scaffolding		
Fire Extinguisher		
Electrical connection		
Ladder		
Maintenance Tool		
Safe Mask		
Face Shield		
Work permit		
Safety Meeting		
Others;		
Health:		
Health facility		
First Aid		
Others;		

Issued by ;

_____
Safety Officer/ Health Officer

Noted by ;

_____
Project Manager

Received by ;

_____
Contractor / Seller

Date Received ;

_____

Company Address :
Telephone :
Fax :
Email : info@
Website: www.

Non Compliance Action (NCA) - Safety and Health

Date Prepared: 02/28/15	**Template ID:** MCT-EHS-002

Project	Name of the Project	**Revision :** 000	**Pages :** 1 of 1
Project Package	Name of the package / phase of the project		
Project Location	Name of the location of the project	**Reference No. :** CM-PEC-D-0047-2015	

Contractor's/Seller's Company Name Company A	**Contractor's/Seller's Name : In charge** Engineer X **Role :** Project Manager
NOTICE NO. 001	**Scope / Work Package / Requirement:**	**Reference :**(Contract provision and others)

Corrective / Preventive Action

No.	Description	Action	Date of Completion	Inspector / Consultant's Comment
1				

Certified by;

_____ / Date _____
Contractor's Quality Control

Verified by;

_____ / Date _____
Contractor's Construction Manager

Received / Approved;

_____ / Date _____
Inspector / Consultant

Noted by;

_____ / Date _____
Project Manager

Step 5

Closing

STEP 5 : CLOSING

Closing is the fifth and last step in managing projects with the purpose of formally completing the contractual obligation and the project or project phase ,This assures that all processes from established project management plan are completed to close the project phase or project .

Flow Chart - Project Management process is not always sequential or performed in identical sequence.

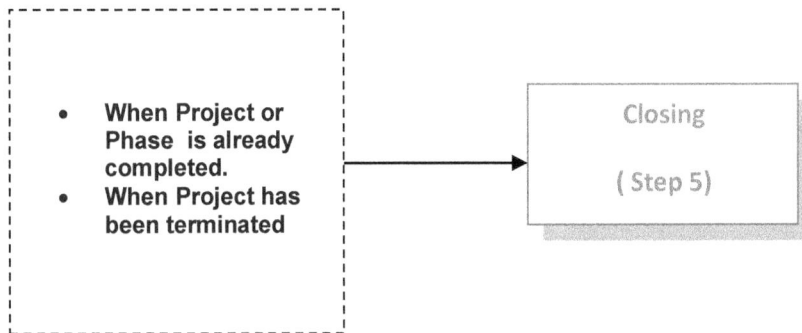

Mapping:

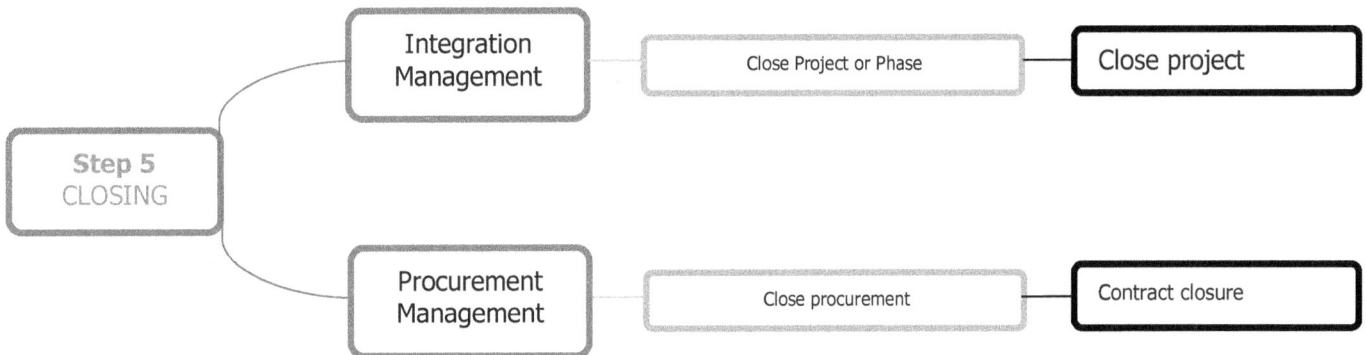

CLOSING PROJECT OR PHASE

The closing project or phase involves checking, verifying, and finalizing the project activities based on established project management processes. All projects must have a formal close out process, whether it is terminated or accepted. This document is being created during the fifth step of managing projects.

Template : Close project

CONTRACT CLOSURE

Contract closure refers to the phase where contract must be closed, including all the information gathered like contract changes, payment records, and performance on the scope, quality, schedule, and cost. This information should be verified and submitted as they will be used in evaluating contractors for future contacts. This document is to be created during the fifth of managing projects.

Template : Contract Closure

Company Address :
Telephone :
Fax :
Email : info@
Website : www.

Close Project

		Date Prepared: 02/28/15	Template ID: CT-I-001
Project	Name of the Project	**Revision:** 000	**Pages:** 1 of 2
Project Package	Name of the package / phase of the project		
Project Location	Name of the location of the project	**Reference No.:** CM-PEC-D-0088-2015	

PROJECT DESCRIPTION:

Description	Cost		Schedule	
	Planned	Actual	Planned	Completed

CONTRACT

			DESCRIPTION				
Category	Contract ID	Number of Pages	Date		Recipient		
			Prepared	Received by Vendor	Name	Role	Organization

	REVISION		
ID	Description		Approval Date

DELIVERABLES:

ID	Category	Deliverables	Acceptance Detail		Comments
			Date	Reference	

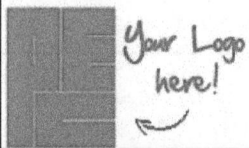

Close Project

Company Address :
Telephone :
Fax :
Email : info@
Website : www.

Date Issue : 02/28/15	Pages : 2 of 2
Reference No.: CM-PEC-D-0088-2015	
Revision No. : 000	

Your Logo here!

PROJECT PERFORMANCE ANALYSIS

Technical	
Scope	
Schedule	
Cost	
Quality	
Requirements	

Others	
Decision making	
Issues	
Communication	

Approvals:

Pier Engineering and Consultants   **P.E.C School**

By: By:

_____

Pier John
Project Manager

_____   _____

Alexander Thomas   **Richard Ramos**
Vice President   President

	Contract Closure	**Date Prepared:** 02/28/15	**Template ID:** CT-P-001
Project	Name of the Project	**Revision:** 000	**Pages:** 1 of 3
Project Package	Name of the package / phase of the project		
Project Location	Name of the location of the project	**Reference No.:** CM-PEC-D-0089-2015	

Company Address:
Telephone:
Fax:
Email: info@
Website: www.

Your Logo here!

SUPPLIER / VENDOR PERFORMANCE ANALYSIS

Technical	
Scope	
Schedule	
Cost	
Quality	
Requirements	
Others	
Decision making	
Issues	
Communication	

	Company Address : Telephone : Fax : Email : info@ Website : www.
Contract Closure	**Date Issue :** 02/28/15 **Pages :** 2 of 3
	Reference No. : CM-PEC-D-0089-2015
	Revision No. : 000

FOR IMPROVEMENT

Technical	
Category	**Corrective Action**
Scope	
Schedule	
Cost	
Quality	
Requirements	
Others	
Category	**Corrective Action**
Decision making	
Issues	
Communication	

Contract Closure

CONTRACT DESCRIPTION:

Category	Contract ID	Number of Pages	Date		Recipient		
			Prepared	Received by Vendor	Name	Role	Organization

CONTRACT CHANGES:

ID	Description	Approval Date

CONTRACT PAYMENTS:

| Payment Number | Date | | Claimed / Bill Amount | Amount | Date (Payment Date) |
	Forwarded by Vendor	Evaluated / Checked		Approved (Amount to be received)	

Approval:

Pier Engineering and Consultants   **P.E.C School**

By: By:

_____   _____   _____

Pier John   **Alexander Thomas**   **Richard Ramos**
Project Manager   Vice President   President

Your Logo here!

Reconciled Claim

			Date Prepared : 09/01/13
Template ID:	CT-CL-001		
Pages :	1 of 1		

Project	Name of the Project	Revision : 000
Project Package	Name of the package / phase of the project	Reference No. :
Project Location	Name of the location of the project	CM:PEC-D-0095-2013

Claim No.	Category / WBS	Claim and Description	Consultant's Estimate	Contractor's Estimate	Reconciled Amount / Quantity	Comments / Justification
1		Force Majeure , 10 Days Time Extension	9 days	10 days	9 days	
2						
3						
4						
5						
6						
7						
8						
9						

Contractor :

Project Owner

Consultant:

www.PierEngineeringandConsultants.com

Manage Templates and Documents the Easy Way.

You can easily manage your entire project templates and documents as easy as shown below!.

Let's have the Step 1 : Initiating (Initiate your project)

The first part of the document is the step *templates (initiating templates)* , as you can see below, this is your controlling documents, where in you can log templates and documents with this specific step (step 1) . This is your document that is generally kept in your main office or company management files, provide a copy in your site files that has to be maintained by your document controller, some companies treated this as a confidential document.

Issuing date is also important for the document history.

Your company detail here! like logo , contacts ,etc.

When your document comprises of several pages, it's good to have a page numbers for easy tracking and monitoring.

Construction Management Toolkit

PIER ENGINEERING AND CONSULTANTS
Your Logo here!
Project Managers • Consulting Engineers

Step 1 : Initiating

Company Address :
Telephone :
Fax :
Email: info@
Website: www.

Initiating Templates

Date Issue :	Pages :
09/01/13	1 of 6
Template ID : CM-IT	
Revision No. : 000	

CONTROL OF DOCUMENTS

| ID | Category | Description | Revision | | Issue Date |
			Number	Revision Description	
IT-I-001	Initiating Process and Integration Areas	Construction Management Contract	000	Not Applicable	09/01/13
IT-I-002	Initiating Process and Integration Areas	Project Statement of Work	000	Not Applicable	09/01/13

DOCUMENT DESCRIPTION

Create your unique ID for your Templates. Here, it is CM – IT , CM for Construction Management Division, or you can use PM as Project Management Division, when your company have different divisions, it's important to put your divisions for quick identification of the documents and IT is for Initiating Templates, meaning , this document is being used and done in the initiating process or the step 1.

IT-I-001 : IT is for Initiating Templates, I is for Integration as shown in the category, meaning this document, Construction Management Contract is being created in the step 1 or initiating and under Integration process (one of the 13 success keys, 001 is the number of document under this process.

Note : You can tailor or edit these initials, codes and identification based on your choice or company preference, what is important here is that, you can easily distinguish what type of document, where to use, what steps and success keys you're in.

183

Here are the templates and documents for Step 1 : Initiating (Initiate your project)

> **IT-I-001 :** IT means this construction management contract is being created and provided in the step 1 or initiating process, I is for Integration Management, meaning this document is for step 1 under Integration management and a first or number one (001) in this process.

4.0 Templates

Number	Form	Template ID	Number of pages
1	Construction Management Contract	IT-I-001	1
2	Project Statement of Work	IT-I-002	2
3	Project Charter	IT-I-003	5
4	Stakeholder Registry	IT-COM-001	1

www.ConstructionProjectManagementPro.com

> **IT-COM-001 :** IT means this stakeholder registry is being created and provided in the step 1 or initiating process, COM is for Communication Management, meaning this document is for step 1 under communication management and a first or number one (001) in this process.

IT - Initiating Process or our Step 1
I - Integration Management (one of the 13 success keys)
COM – Communication Management (one of the 13 success keys)
001 and others – Document number for every success keys.

Note : You can tailor or edit these initials, codes and identification based on your choice or company preference, what is important here is that, you can easily distinguish what type of document, where to use, what steps and success keys you're in.

FOR LETTERS, DOCUMENTS AND REPORTS

CM - for Division or Construction Management Division (CM Division), you can use PM as Project Management Division

PEC - Your company name

D – This is a document

0001 – Document number under category of document.

2013 – The year created this document.

IT-I-003 : IT means this project charter is being created and provided in the step 1 or initiating process, I is for Integration Management, meaning this document is for step 1 under Integration management and the third or number three (003) in the document for Integration management.

Construction Management Toolkit

Step 1 : Initiating

Template ID : IT-I-003
Revision : 000

Reference No. : CM-PEC-D-0001-2013

Date : September 01 , 2013
Page 1 of 5

PROJECT CHARTER

1.0 PROJECT DESCRIPTION
This shows a descriptive summary of the project.

The Management of P.E.C. School have noticed the increase of college students every school year and decided to have an additional school building to accommodate the increasing number of enrollees.

D – This is a Document
L - This is a Letter
R – This is a Report

Note : You can tailor or edit these initials, codes and identification based on your choice or company preference, what is important here is that, you can easily distinguish what type of document, where to use, what steps and success keys you're in.

FOR TEMPLATES

As always mentioned in this publication, all Templates and Project Documents has been properly coded and arranged in sequence, see illustration below how it works!.

Project Name and Location - It's perfect to start your Forms, Templates with the name of the project, it's the title of what project you are working for and this template referring for. Location is important also as reference and identification, some projects you can easily remind through location.

Package – This is useful to identify what specifically you are working with. Let's say the project is a large Mall and your specific project package is only the foundation works (bored piling works etc), as a project manager of foundation project, you can easily separate your specific project package with the entire

TEMPLATE ID : IT-COM-001 -

- ➤ **IT** - means this Stakeholder Registry is being created and provided in the step 1 or initiating process.
- ➤ **COM** - is for Communication Management, meaning this document is for step 1 under Communication Management.
- ➤ **001-** Is the first or the number one in the document or file for communication management.

Construction Management Toolkit   Step 1 - Initiating

Company Address :
Telephone :
Fax :
Email : info@
Website www.

Stakeholder Registry		Date Prepared : 09/01/13	Template ID: IT-COM-001
Project	Name of the Project	Revision : 000	Pages : 1 of 1
Project Package	Name of the package / phase of the project		
Project Location	Name of the location of the project	Reference No. : CM-PEC-D-0002-2013	

Your Logo here

Reference No. – This is your reference number for every specific document or a template.

CM-PEC-D-0002-2013 :

CM : Construction Management Division, some companies have different divisions, like CM, Design Division or you can use **PM** as Project Management Division etc.

PEC is for your company initial or name

D is for a document, this template is a kind of Document.

0002 – Is the number of document, meaning the stakeholder template is the second template for a Document and not a Letter or Report.

2013 – The year when did you created this type of document.

USEFUL ABBREVIATION AS TAG OR A CODE TO EASILY MANAGE YOUR PROJECT DOCUMENTS.

➢ **5 Easy Steps**

1. **IT**   :   Initiating Templates
2. **PT**   :   Planning Templates
3. **ET**   :   Executing Templates
4. **MCT**   :   Monitoring and Controlling Templates
5. **CT**   :   Closing Templates

➢ **13 Success Keys**

1. **I**   :   Integration Management
2. **SC**   :   Scope Management
3. **T**   :   Time Management
4. **C**   :   Cost Management
5. **Q**   :   Quality Management
6. **HR**   :   Human Resource Management
7. **COM**   :   Communication Management
8. **R**   :   Risk Management
9. **P**   :   Procurement Management

Note : You can tailor or edit these initials, codes and identification based on your choice or company preference, what is important here is that, you can easily distinguish what type of document, where to use, what steps and success keys you're in.

www.PierEngineeringandConsultants.com
The Company for Project Managers and Consulting Engineers.

FOR CONSTRUCTION PROJECT

www.ConstructionProjectManagementPro.com
Get Your Free Templates ,Flow charts, Articles, Examples, videos for construction projects and Learn the ins and outs of Construction Management.

www.ConstructionManagementToolkit.com
The Complete and Step-by-Step Guide to Construction Management, You will discover all the processes involved in project management for construction projects , from 5 Easy Steps , Templates, Form, Flowcharts, Example, Tips and Tricks To 13 Success Keys, all are arranged in sequence and all templates and documents are fully customizable.

www.Facebook.com/constructionprojectmanagementpro
Like Us on FACEBOOK to get the latest update, free tools announcement and more..

> As a purchaser of this book, you will also receive an electronic file through email of all the templates and documents for you to personalize and customize in your own preference and liking.
>
> Just send us an email and we will send files and other bonuses.

As promised shown on our website…

YOUR FREE
PROJECT MANAGEMENT
TOOLS
($ 147.00 Value)

This Includes:

✓ Legal Document: Project Management Services Contract

✓ Bid Conference: Pre-bid Conference Presentation Documents

As a purchaser of this book, you will also receive an electronic file through email of all the templates and documents for you to personalize and customize in your own preference and liking.

Just send us an email and we will send files and other bonuses.